Learn Spanish:

A Fast and Easy Guide for Beginners to Learn Conversational Spanish

Free membership into the Mastermind Self Development Group!

For a limited time, you can join the Mastermind Self Development Group for free! You will receive videos and articles from top authorities in self development as well as a special group only offers on new books and training programs. There will also be a monthly member only draw that gives you a chance to win any book from your Kindle wish list!

If you sign up through this link
http://www.mastermindselfdevelopment.com/specialreport you will also get a special free report on the Wheel of Life. This report will give you a visual look at your current life and then take you through a series of exercises that will help you plan what your perfect life looks like. The workbook does not end there; we then take you through a process to help you plan how to achieve that perfect life. The process is very powerful and has the potential to change your life forever. Join the group now and start to change your life!
http://www.mastermindselfdevelopment.com/specialreport

Table of Contents

Introduction

Congratulations on downloading Learn Spanish: A Fast and Easy Guide for Beginners to Learn Conversational Spanish and thank you for doing so.

The following chapters will discuss how you can start speaking Spanish fast. This book is based around a method that I've developed and curated alongside and based off of some of the most prolific language learners and educators of the modern age.

Why learn Spanish? Well, I'm sure that if you picked up this book, you already had a reason, but it's worth going a bit more into it anyway. You should learn Spanish because, simply put, it's a rich language.

Over the last several centuries, Spanish has been across multiple continents and forged connections between all of them. Spanish has persisted as a linguistic force since the Spanish empire began to cover the world over. The language spoken now isn't quite the same as the language spoken in the 15th century on the first voyage to the new world, but the similarities between that variety of Spanish and the modern day variety of Spanish sets you up for libraries worth of literature from all over the world in the Spanish language.

What's more is the sheer beauty of the fact that Spanish, since it's covered the world over, has taken in a number of influences from other languages. Through its journey starting as a mere dialectical splinter of Vulgar Latin (the version of Latin spoken by the general populace of the Roman Republic and the Roman Empire), Spanish has picked up plenty of influences from all kinds of different languages and cultures, most notably from Arabic during the Arab occupation of Spain from the 700s to around the thirteenth century, but also from the Goths, the Basques, the Native Americans, and the Celts.

So in other words, when you learn Spanish, you're setting yourself up to be involved in learning a whole wealth of cultural and historical information in what is a relatively passive manner. That sheer attachment to history is one of the most beautiful things about learning language in general.

However, there are a great number of reasons otherwise for which you might learn Spanish. The growth of the Latin American population and the dissemination of Latin American culture into the United States provides an excellent opportunity in two ways. Firstly, you will inevitably be a more attractive candidate for various careers from a perspective of qualifications. Your ability to speak Spanish will make you an asset in more ways than you can possibly fathom, and a huge number of companies will be lining up in order to get you to work with them, especially if you're specialized in another manner too. Secondly, you'll have opened the door to talking to a whole new set of people. No longer will you be relegated to speaking simply to people who know and understand English;

rather, you'll be able to speak to and with people from the culturally beautiful continents of South America and Central America and the wonderful Latin American people. It will also enable you to go to travel to Spain with ease and talk to numerous people who are native Spanish speakers and, more importantly, natives to the *region*, which will most certainly help you to understand the culture, customs, and realities of the place that you're in.

I've already mentioned how Spanish is a language with an absolutely colossal reach, and with that in mind, I feel as though it's necessary to make a certain stipulation. Just like the English spoken in the United States, the English spoken in Australia, and the English spoken in England are vastly different, likewise is the Spanish of Spain, the Spanish of Mexico, and the Spanish of, say, Argentina. They're different in manner of accent and dialect and some basic things, such as the usage of "vosotros" in Castilian Spanish (*Castellano*), or the Spanish of mainland Spain, where instead "ustedes" is used in Latin American Spanish. There's also the fact that certain dialects use the pronoun *vos*, which is generally never used otherwise and sounds rather booky and antiquated in the same way that using the pronoun *thou* sounds in English.

There are plenty of books on this subject on the market, thanks again for choosing this one! Every effort was made to ensure it is full of as much useful information as possible, please enjoy! I can guarantee that by the end of this book, you're going to feel comfortable speaking and reading Spanish.

Chapter 1: Spanish - how does it work?

In the United States, there's an institution called the *Foreign Service Institute*. What they do is train people, generally federal agents such as diplomats, in order to be prepared to go overseas in order to promote United States interests. They provide a huge number of courses in over seventy foreign languages and are one of the authorities on language learning in the United States.

The Foreign Service Institute has a list of languages cut into categories based upon how difficult they are for native English speakers to pick up and learn. Languages such as Arabic, Chinese, and Japanese rank among the hardest, being placed in category V: languages which are "exceptionally difficult for native English speakers."

Languages such as Danish, French, and indeed Spanish place, fortunately, in the simplest ranking: category I, which contains languages closely related to language.

A given language makes their way into this category in several ways. For example, they might share similar sentence structure and grammar to English. On top of that, they might share a lot of common vocabulary (many of the languages in category I developed alongside each other.)

What does this mean for you as a student learner of Spanish? Primarily, it means that you should have an easy enough time getting acquainted with the language and finding your way around it.

In fact, there are a laundry list of similarities between Spanish and English. Take this lightly, however. I've said it a million times before across multiple books: you shouldn't focus on the similarities. There are a few reasons for this.

The first major reason for not getting caught up on minor similarities is that eventually you're going to run into what the French call *faux amis* - "false friends." These are words which sound like they would mean one thing in English but mean a totally different thing in Spanish. Take, for example, the word "éxito." This is a Spanish word, and when an English speaker looks at it, they assume boldly that it means "exit", because, well, it looks like it means "exit". The Spanish word for "exit", though, is "salida" - the word "éxito" actually means "success"! Very, very different word.

There are a huge number more true cognates - words which mean exactly what it sounds like between Spanish and English - than false cognates. But that doesn't mean that it's not too easy to hear very common false cognates and think that they're a certain English word when they're not. This stems from two problems: first, it stems from the person making the bold assumption that English and Spanish must have something in common simply because a given word sounds similarly. This is nowhere *near* the truth, as it frankly shouldn't ever be. And secondly, it stems from a lack of looking at the word contextually and trying to truly figure out what it means given the other words in the sentence. The idea of "context" is your best friend when doing any sort of immersion based language learning, so learning to use it at its most appropriate and as often as you possibly can is wholly essential.

The second major reason for not getting caught up on minor similarities is that, frankly, every language has a lot more in common than things that set them apart. Perhaps not in the context of vocabulary - and there are also things among various languages which are particularly niche and neat, such as the Japanese and Korean languages' ideas of "topic markers" - but at the end of the day, languages are far more *similar* than they are different. After all, what is language, really? Language is simply a method of using our ability to speak in order to transmit and process information between one another. It's the apex of human cooperation. In that respect, every language is serving the same purpose: transmittance and processing of given tidbits of information. And all information has something in common: the rational devolution of a sentence into smaller pseudo-concepts. For example, different languages may place them differently, but every single language has a mechanism for denoting the bare linguistic essentials, like subjects (the thing around which the sentence is formed), actions (the things which the subject undertakes), objects (the thing which receives or acts as recipient of the action), as well as various modifiers in order to further and better describe things.

So to get stuck on the similarities between Spanish and English is absolutely absurd, because to point out the similarities is to say things such as "Spanish and English both have *objects*", "Spanish and English both have *pronouns*", and "Spanish and English both have some degree of Latin derivation due to their historical basis from mainland Europe." That's practically useless information in the grand context of language learning.

The things which actually matter in the context of language learning are found in the *differences*. The same basic mechanisms will persist, albeit manifested differently.

So what are the differences between English and Spanish? Well, despite the similarity of the two languages, they're numerous.

For one, Spanish has a very different system of pronunciation to English. It's far more regular but also a fair bit more nuanced in the specific sounds. With the espoused regularity of Spanish pronunciation comes a fair amount of adjustment from our English alphabet where a given letter can stand in for any number of different sounds. What this essentially means is that Spanish offers a far more rigid system of pronunciation which makes it easier to speak and learn, but it also means that you'll simultaneously have to undo some of the pronunciation consistencies that you've subconsciously learned while speaking English, which can be a lot easier said than done. Anyhow. we'll go more into the specific pronunciation of words in the second chapter.

Lesson one: Gendered nouns

Another way that Spanish differs is that it treats adverbs and adjectives far differently than English does. This might not sound terribly menacing at first, but it can definitely be difficult to keep up with early on in you're learning. The reason that it's so weird is because Spanish has something called *gendered nouns*. I'm introducing this concept to you early because it's the one which is bound to trip you up first and, as such, it deserves to be the first concept which you really work with.

Spanish applies genders to every single noun. For example, the word for *banana* is masculine (*plátano)*, while the word for *table* is feminine (*mesa)*.

So what does this mean? Does this mean that tables are meant for women and bananas are meant for men? That a woman eating a banana implies that she's doing something not "ladylike"? No, not at all.

The concept of gendered nouns is a purely grammatical concept and has nothing to do with any kind of innate masculinity or femininity of a noun. It's actually a concept which dates back to vulgar Latin, where there were three articles (we'll talk about those in a moment) known as *ille, illa,* and *illud*. Well, they were actually demonstrative adjectives, but that's another discussion entirely. These would be used by the common people in order to refer to specific instances of a noun, and which one you use would largely depend upon the ending sound of the word which came before it. This is a concept known as "vowel harmony". In other words, the concept of grammatical gender is wholly and entirely a solely linguistic concept and has more to do with the harmony of certain phrases than any sort of innate characteristics of the object deciding whether it is "male" or "female". There actually used to be another gender, the *neuter* gender, which was just a third grammatical category for nouns. This gender, however, was dropped with time.

Lesson two: Articles

Articles in Spanish act rather differently to those in English. They correspond specifically to the noun in question in terms of gender and plurality.

English doesn't do this so much. To compare this sort of difference, let's first analyze English's article system.

In English, there are two articles: *the* and either *a* or *an* depending on whether the next work begins with a vowel or a consonant sound. *The* is what's called a definite article, and *a/an* are what are called indefinite articles.

A *definite article* is an article which has a direct correspondence to a specifically stated object in space. For example, take the sentence "have you turned *the* television on today?" Because of the phrasing of this sentence, you can assume that they're referring to one very specific television which would either be denoted by context (perhaps you're all in the living room and the television won't turn on) or by a clause which specifically denotes which object is being referred to. ("Did you turn the television *in the living room* on today?")

An *indefinite article* is an article which lacks the specificity of the direct article. That is to say that the *indefinite article* refers to a non-specific instance of an object in space. If somebody were to ask you "have you turned *a* television on today?", you would think it was bizarre - principally because when would somebody ask that question? - but you would also likely say "yes" or "no" depending on whether or not you have indeed turned on *any* given television at some point in the day.

This distinction also exists in Spanish, but it's a bit more nuanced.

Spanish has four different *definite articles* which respond to the gender and plurality of an object. For these examples, I'm going to reuse the *banana* and *table* words.

The Spanish definite articles are as follows:

El - singular masculine definite

La - singular feminine definite

Los - plural masculine or mixed definite

Las - plural feminine definite

When I say the "masculine or mixed definite", I mean that if you have a group of people that are of either gender, or objects which are of either gender, then you should use "los". If every given object to which you're directly referring is feminine, then and only then should you use "las".

Spanish also has four different *indefinite articles*. The Spanish articles can broadly translate to either "a", "an", or "some" dependent upon the context.

The Spanish indefinite articles are as follows:

Un - singular masculine indefinite

Una - singular feminine indefinite

Unos- plural masculine or mixed indefinite

Unas - plural feminine indefinite

So how would I relate these to the two nouns I already know at this point? Simple. Let's run through a few basic exercises. Quick reminder that the term for *banana* is *el plátano* and the term for *table* is *la mesa*. Plurality in Spanish works by simply appending an *s*, just like it works in English.

1. Translate "the tables".
2. Translate "some bananas".

3. Translate "a table".
4. Translate "the bananas."
   Your answers should have come out as follows:

1. *Las mesas*
2. *Unos plátanos*
3. *Una mesa*
4. *Los plátanos*

The reason that they come out like that is pretty plain. There's not a whole lot going on here, the main things to take away from this lesson is that nouns have specific genders in Spanish, as they do in other Romance languages and a quarter of languages in the world, actually.

There's one more problem we encounter here: the *uncountable nouns* issue. For example, you can eat three peaches, but you can't drink three waters. In the case of an uncountable noun - usually a liquid, but could be any variety of things - you're to not use an article at all.

Lesson three: Subject pronouns

So at the moment, what we're trying to do is form very basic Spanish sentences with a really cursory amount of knowledge that will create a baseline level of Spanish for you to work with going forward.

Sentences in any given language have three basic components, at the minimum: a *subject*, an *object*, and a *verb*. We've covered the basics of introducing objects to your Spanish by covering the bare essentials of nouns and noun gendering. However, in order to do a lot more with this lesson, we really have to critically analyze the whole concept of *subject pronouns* before we can really make our way onto verbs. Spanish verbs are far, *far* more complex than English ones (despite having relatively simpler conjugation rules than a large number of other concurrent Romance languages).

Subject pronouns form the very basis of the most basic sentences. If you don't know what a pronoun is, it is essentially the word which replaces the subject in a sentence.

We make extensive use of this in English, because we really like to talk in the first person. What I mean by this is that if somebody's name were John, and you were having a discussion with him, it would sound terribly awkward if he said "John is going to the store later. John is excited, because John is going to get the stuff to make curry." That simply doesn't work for the way that we structure sentences. We far prefer to *change* those words to the first-person subject pronoun in order to make it sound more accurate and give more context as to who is speaking. This makes fundamentally more sense from a linguistic perspective, too. When we say "I", there's no question about who is speaking - you're referring to yourself. So the distinction between the "I" and actually saying your name is totally unnecessary.

Spanish has these distinctions are well. Spanish actually has a few more of these distinctions than we do - I'll get to that in a second.

The Spanish pronouns are as follows:

Yo - I

Tú - You (singular, informal)

Usted - You (singular, formal)

Él - He/It (masculine)

Ella - She/It (feminine)

Nosotros - We

Ustedes - You (plural) (Latin America)

Vosotros - You (plural) (Spain)

Ellos - Male/masculine or mixed gender group

Ellas - Female/feminine group

Remember that we're working with explicitly Latin American Spanish in this book, and as such, we aren't going to really mess around with conjugating the *vosotros* pronoun. There are three key differences from English in this set-up of subject pronouns.

The first major difference is the separation of the *tú* and *usted* informal and formal pronouns. In English, no such distinction exists. In Middle English it did, as the distinction between *thou* and *you*; however, this has faded away with time as *you* has taken precedence. In case you're unfamiliar with informal and formal pronouns: you use the informal when you're speaking to somebody that you know well, such as a family member or friend, or somebody younger than you. You use the formal when you're speaking to somebody in a position of authority over you, or when you're meeting somebody for the first time.

The next major difference is that Spanish has an official verb for the second-person plural. This is another thing that we don't have in English. This entire idea is actually rather foreign to English. This place is filled by colloquial phrases. In the Southern United States, "y'all" fills the niche; in the Northeast, "youse"; in the Midwest, "you guys". There is not, however, a relatively standardized form, nor is there a singular word. (Even "y'all" is a contraction of the phrase "you all".)

The third major difference is that the Spanish don't have a specific word for "it". The reason for this is obvious if you think about it: they don't have a neuter pronoun or neuter gender *at all*. That concept is missing from Spanish completely in modernity. As such, since every item has either a feminine or masculine grammatical gender, it makes perfect sense to simply use the feminine and masculine pronouns in order to refer to it in a way.

The reason that we're spending a while on this topic is so that you're prepared for the next topic, which will be a lot heavier: *verb conjugation*. But for the concept of verb conjugation, you have to have a subject in the first place to conjugate for.

Without further ado, let's move to the next lesson, which no doubt is of astronomical importance.

Lesson four: Basic verb conjugation (-er verbs)

So what is verb conjugation? In English, we have a very simplified form. Verb conjugation is simply the changing of the ending of a given verb, or action word, depending upon the person who's performing it. A lot of the verb conjugation in English has fallen away with time. In its place is only a very simple remnant.

Let's take the verb "*to run*" (this form being called the "infinitive") and conjugate it in the present tense.

I run

You run

He/she/it run**s**

We run

They run

The only form of verb conjugation which occurs in the present tense is the adding of the *-s* to the third person singular form.

This is a very different story from Spanish. Spanish is an absolutely beautiful and expressive language. Along with this comes a huge amount of caveats concerning writing and speaking, though.

The heavy conjugation system, however, does have some bright sides. The fact that verbs end differently depending upon who is speaking means that generally, the subject pronoun can (and will) be dropped altogether. This means that sentences are, of course, far more expressive and clear than they often would be otherwise, while also being more economical.

So how do you conjugate a basic present tense verb in Spanish?

Let's look at this using the verb *comer*, meaning *to eat*.

Comer - *to speak*

Conjugation	Meaning	Pronunciation
Yo com*o*.	I eat.	yoh coh-moh
Tú com*es*.	You eat.	too coh-mehs
Él/ella/usted com*e*.	He/she/you eat.	el/ey-yah/oos-ted coh-meh
Nosotros com*emos*.	We eat.	noh-soh-tros coh-meh-mos
Ellos/Ellas/Ustedes com*en*.	They/they/you all eat.	ey-yohs/ey-yahs/oos-ted-ehs coh-mehn

This gives you a very simple summary of how to conjugate a regular *-er* verb in Spanish. There are two other verb forms, which we'll get to momentarily, as well as a slew of irregular verbs, with what are in fact the most common verbs in the language being irregular. We'll also get to those momentarily.

You'll notice in the conjugation table that depending upon who is speaking, the end of the word would change. This is the bare essence of verb conjugation: changing the word in accordance with who is speaking.

There are a whole host of regular -er verbs that you'll find useful. I'm going to give you the conjugation tables for two more, before giving you a bunch of them to practice with.

Vender - *to sell*

Conjugation	Meaning	Pronunciation
Yo vend*o*.	I sell.	yoh vehn-doh
Tú vend*es*.	You sell.	too vehn-dehs
Él/ella/usted vend*e*.	He/she/you sell.	el/ey-yah/oos-ted vehn-deh
Nosotros vend*emos*.	We sell.	noh-soh-tros vehn-deh-mos
Ellos/Ellas/Ustedes vend*en*.	They/they/you all sell.	ey-yohs/ey-yahs/oos-ted-ehs vehn-dehn

Comprender - *to understand*

Conjugation	Meaning	Pronunciation
Yo comprend*o*.	I understand.	yoh cohm-prehn-doh
Tú comprend*es*.	You understand.	too cohm-prehn-dehs
Él/ella/usted comprend*e*.	He/she/you understand.	el/ey-yah/oos-ted cohm-prehn-dehs
Nosotros comprend*emos*.	We understand.	noh-soh-tros cohm-prehn-mos
Ellos/Ellas/Ustedes comprend*en*.	They/they/you all eat.	ey-yohs/ey-yahs/oos-ted-ehs coh-mehn

By now, you should see a very tangible pattern among these. With that in mind, I'm going to give you a few more super common *-er* verbs before we move on to conjugating *-ar* and *-ir* verbs.

Practice verbs:

- aprender: *to learn*
- beber: *to drink*
- poseer: *to possess* or *to own*
- responder: *to respond* or *to answer*
- ofender: *to offend*
- promete: *to promise*
- someter: *to submit*

Lesson five: Regular verb conjugation with -ar and -ir verbs

With the very basics of verb conjugation out of the way, we can now move onto the other verb forms. As I said, Spanish verb forms tend to take three types: *-er*, *-ar*, or *-ir*. Sadly, a lot of the most common verbs are irregular and don't follow traditional conjugation, but that's just what happens when you have a lot of people speaking a language over a lot of space and saying these words constantly: uniformity falls away to slang as the natural process of linguistic evolution is exacerbated by constant usage. But with that said, the vast wealth of Spanish verbs are indeed regular, they just don't happen to be quite as common. Anyway, we'll get to regular verbs in the next lesson.

The first thing that we're going to cover here is the concept of conjugating *-ar* verbs. We're going to start this process out with the verb *hablar*, meaning "to speak".

Hablar - *to speak*

Conjugation	Meaning	Pronunciation
Yo habl*o*.	I speak.	yoh ah-bloh
Tú habl*as*.	You speak.	too ah-blahs
Él/ella/usted habl*a*.	He/she/you speak.	el/ey-yah/oos-ted ah-blah
Nosotros habl*amos*.	We speak.	noh-soh-tros ah-blah-mos
Ellos/Ellas/Ustedes habl*an*.	They/they/you all speak.	ey-yohs/ey-yahs/oos-ted-ehs ah-blahn

You'll notice that a lot of these conjugations are superbly similar to the same conjugations for *-er* verbs, and you'd be right to notice that. The only major noticeable difference between the two is that these verbs, of course, take an *a* in place of the *e*.

-ir verbs act similarly and, in fact, aren't that different either. In fact, their conjugation is exactly the same as *-er* verbs, except for the "Nosotros" form. Observe what I mean as we conjugate the verb *discutir*, meaning "to discuss".

Discutir - *to discuss*

Conjugation	Meaning	Pronunciation
Yo discut*o*.	I discuss.	yoh dees-cooh-toh
Tú discut*es*.	You discuss.	too dees-cooh-tehs
Él/ella/usted discut*e*.	He/she/you discuss.	el/ey-yah/oos-ted dees-cooh-teh
Nosotros discut*imos*.	We discuss.	noh-soh-tros dees-cooh-tee-mos
Ellos/Ellas/Ustedes discut*en*.	They/they/you all discuss.	ey-yohs/ey-yahs/oos-ted-ehs dees-coo-tehn

Indeed, you'll see that there's little to no difference in the conjugation of these *-ir* verbs in the present tense than conjugating *-er* verbs in the present tense aside from the *nosotros* form.

By now, you've conjugated verbs in all forms, so the only thing you can do now is practice. That's how one genuinely and truly picks up skill in verb conjugation. At first, it will be ugly and very much not fun, but after a little practice, you'll be able to do it with absolute ease.

Here are some verbs with which you can practice your conjugating.

-ar verbs:

- caminar: *to walk*
- esperar: *to hope*
- comprar: *to buy*
- ayudar: *to help*
- viajar: *to travel*
- trabajar: *to work*

-ir verbs:

- vivir: *to live*
- debatir: *to debate*
- describir: *to describe*
- unir: *to unite*
- escribir: *to write*
- reunir: *to meet*

Of course there's an endless wealth of Spanish verbs that you can work with, and a little personal research certainly wouldn't be out of the question if you were so inclined. You know how to conjugate these verbs now, and it's on your pto practice it.

Lesson six: Irregular verbs, part one

The hardest part of coming to a new Romance language is frankly not learning conjugation. I've studied quite a few and conjugation comes relatively easy at this point. After all, it's a very finite system with little that ever really changes about it. No, the hardest part is totally and completely getting used to each language's irregular verbs and the numerous idiomatic ways in which they use their irregular verbs.

Given that this is a Spanish book, I won't give you the details all about, say, French or Italian's conjugation system. However, with the fact that it's a Spanish book established, we do need to move on to talking about how to actually conjugate and use these verbs.

The first one that we really need to cover is **ser**, which translates to "to be". It's actually one of two state of being verbs that Spanish has, and between it and the other verb *estar*, the general bases of the verb "to be" as it's used in English are covered.

Of course, the downside of having two verbs for something we represent with one in English is that, naturally, it's more efficient and expressive, but this also comes with the fact that for native English speakers it can be a terribly big adjustment to make linguistically. If you aren't used to representing these sort of ideas using two distinct verbs, then it's going to be a very odd thing for you to start to do so.

So with that said, when does one actually venture out and try to use *ser*? There are a few situations which call for *ser* specifically. The first time in which you'd use *ser* is in situations which specifically refer to things which are essential to you or somebody else's identity. These include things such as any physical description, your personality and your sense of character, the country that you're from, the race that you are, the gender that you are, what you do for a living, and what any given thing in general is made of.

Another time that you'd use *ser* is to donate any given thing which occurs or takes place at a point in time, such as dates, seasons, events, and time in general.

So how do we conjugate *ser*? Since *ser* is irregular, it'd most likely be easy for you starting out to simply try to remember the following conjugation table, which will come naturally anyhow with practice:

Ser - *to be*

Conjugation	Meaning	Pronunciation
Yo *soy*.	I am.	yoh soy
Tú *eres*.	You are.	too eh-res
Él/ella/usted *es*.	He/she/you are.	el/ey-yah/oos-ted es
Nosotros *somos*.	We are.	noh-soh-tros soh-mos
Ellos/Ellas/Ustedes *son*.	They/they/you are.	ey-yohs/ey-yahs/oos-ted-ehs sohn

So if you wanted to say, for example, "I'm from the United States", that's an intrinsic quality and description of you, so you would use *ser* here. "I'm from the United States" is a nifty sentence because it can actually translate quite directly from English into Spanish.

Yo *soy* de <u>los Estados Unidos</u>.*

I *am* from <u>the United States</u>.

** bear in mind that in conventional spoken Spanish, the "yo" would be dropped since the person who is speaking is implied directly through the verb conjugation.*

So with all of that noted, when would we use the other word for *to be*, "estar"? Well, there are a few different cases in which you would use *estar*. It really depends. A good way to remember the usage of *estar* is the following rhyme often taught in high schools: "how you feel and where you are, that is when you use *estar*."

That rhyme, though simple, is not terribly far off base at all. The first usage of *estar* is, indeed, where you are. *Estar*'s principle usage is "emotional and physical states of being". These are temporary things like moods or appearances. This can make quite a massive difference. If you were to say:

Soy enojado.

Wherein *enojado* means "angry", you'd be essential telling the world that you're a very angry person in general. You'd be saying that anger is an essential personality description of you, a permanent fixture of description for you. This is fine if you're, for example, an angsty teenager who is mad at the world or popular multi-million selling rap artist Eminem, but otherwise, you most likely should use *estar*. Using *estar* here makes a world of difference. When used with emotion or states of being, *estar* can often also stand in for the word "feel" in English: *estar enojado* means "to be feeling angry", which removes the existential burden of being an angry person in general off of your back.

Estar is also the verb that you're supposed to use in order to indicate your location at a given time. Use *estar* in order to say that you're in either this place or that. You can use *estar* in order to denote the location of both people and of things.

So into the belly of the beast: how do we conjugate *estar*? Like so:

Estar - *to be (states of being)*

Conjugation	Meaning	Pronunciation
Yo *estoy*.	I am/feel.	yoh es-toy
Tú *estás*.	You are/feel.	too es-tahs
Él/ella/usted *está*.	He/she/you are/feel.	el/ey-yah/oos-ted es-tah
Nosotros *estamos*.	We are/feel.	noh-soh-tros es-tah-mos
Ellos/Ellas/Ustedes *están*.	They/they/you all are/feel.	ey-yohs/ey-yahs/oos-ted-ehs es-tahn

The distinction between *soy* and *estar* isn't terribly difficult to ascertain once you've got a grasp on it, but it will take two things in order for you to understand nuances like this fully: the first is *practice*. In order to understand how to use these verbs correctly - and indeed, a great number of Spanish words and idioms and phrases in general - you're going to have to practice using them correct. The second is *immersion*. Without proper immersion, you're well doomed. Luckily, modern society makes it very easy to simulate immersion in several different ways, such as watching television shows in other languages or signing up to talk to people who speak another language via services such as italki. Immersion is what allows you to hear the various uses of different phrases and understand how certain ideas and words are used in the context of another language.

Lesson seven: Tenses, part one

There's one more important distinction and usage of *estar* that we haven't really covered yet. Aside from its obvious appearance in Spanish idioms, there's a very important tense that we need to talk about: the present progressive.

Depending on your experiences with other languages, you may or may not be familiar with the common usage of the present progressive. Some languages don't have a present progressive tense in common use, such as French and Danish. English, however, takes great advantage of the present progressive tense.

What the present progressive tense does is indicate an action which is in the process of occurring. For example, if you were studying French, you might run into the sentence "Je chante". This can carry a meaning of either "I sing" in a general sense, or it can carry the meaning of "I am *currently* singing." French has this in a colloquial sense (the phrase "être en train de *verb*" can indicate an ongoing process) but in literature and more formal usage, there is no real equivalent for the present progressive - the simple present tense is used.

In Spanish and English, however, we make this distinction. For example, the phrase "I eat meat" would generally mean that somebody eats meat as a general part of their diet, but by inclusion of the verb "to be" and morphing "eat" into its gerund (the noun form of a verb), we can form the sentence "I *am* eat*ing* meat." which indicates that as we speak, we are eating meat.

Spanish has a very similar system. They too use *estar*, meaning of course "to be", in order to form the present progressive. as well as forming a present participle much like we form gerunds.

The way that the present participle is formed in Spanish is by looking at what kind of verb it is. If it's an *-er* or *-ir* verb, you just drop the ending and replace it with *-iendo*. This means that a verb like *someter*, which we discovered earlier means "to submit", would take on the form *somiendo*. For *-ar* verbs, what you would do is drop the *-ar* ending and replace it with *-ando*. So the verb *trabajar*, again meaning "to work", would become *trabajando*.

So depending upon who is speaking, one would simply conjugate *estar* to the correct form and then stick the present participle after it.

Let's practice! Translate the following:

1) I am working. (trabajar)
2) She is learning. (aprender)
3) You are writing. (escribir)
   Your responses should have been as follows:

1) *Estoy trabajando.*
2) *Está aprendiendo.*
3) *Estás escribiendo.*

Are you seeing how this works, a tad? It's a relatively simple tense to form but it can be bizarre.

When you try to form present participles, remember also that not all verbs are created equal. Some, because they have endings which would make appending *-iendo* or *-ando* sound strange, don't have regular endings in the present participle. Be wary of this and, as always, be sure to research constantly as you learn. There's little more important than testing your limits, but being sure that the way you're testing them is correct is definitely up there.

Lesson eight: Working with "haber"

There are quite a few irregular verbs in Spanish. Somewhere close to around 34 percent. And the most common verbs are more likely to be irregular, too, go figure. For example, of the fifteen most common verbs in Spanish, *thirteen out of fifteen* can be described as irregular. It's absolutely absurd.

What this means for you as a language learner is that you are going to have to dedicate yourself to not only knowing normal regular verb conjugations but to knowing how to conjugate the irregular verbs, as well. Some of them have fall into patterns which are easily recognized, such as *hacer* and *decir* or *tener* and *poner*. Others, not so much.

Because of all of this, it can be rather difficult to really know where to start. The answer is that there is not quite a "right" place to start - it's just something that you're going to have to learn as you go on and attempt to use the words or hear the words used.

However, I do think that it's certainly sensible to start with the most *common* irregular verbs first, because you're far more likely to use them on a sentence to sentence basis. So with that said, let's start working a bit more with these irregular verbs and practicing them so that they get mentally tucked away for later use whenever you may need them once more.

The only other major irregular verb that we're going to work with in the context of this book is *haber*. This verb means roughly "to have" (though not in the sense of possessing something - for that purpose, you would use *poseder* instead). *Haber* means "to have" in the sense of the past, which we'll get to in a bit when we discuss more tenses.

Aside from this case (usage as an auxiliary verb), *haber* primarily is used in two other contexts. We'll discuss that after conjugating. Here's how you'd conjugate *haber*.

Haber - *to have*

Conjugation	Meaning	Pronunciation
Yo he.	I have.	yoh eh
Tú has.	You have.	too ahs
Él/ella/usted ha *or* hay.	He/she/you have.	el/ey-yah/oos-ted ah *or* eye
Nosotros hemos.	We have.	noh-soh-tros eh-mos
Ellos/Ellas/Ustedes han *or* hay.	They/they/you all have.	ey-yohs/ey-yahs/oos-ted-ehs ahn *or* eye

So, *haber* when not used to construct the perfect tense usually is used in one of two manners.

Firstly, it may be used in order to say "there is". It's not a direct translation, but if you think about it, it doesn't need to be. "There is" is a nonsensical impersonal phrase. All that it directly implies is the fact that something *is*, in the something *exists*. So *hay* is as much an equivalent phrase in Spanish as *il y a* is in French.

This is simple enough. Let's take that word for banana again, *plátano*. If we wanted to say there is a banana on the table. We'd do this like so:

There's a banana on the table.

Hay uno plátano en la mesa.

It works similarly for doubled objects where we'd otherwise use "There are" as opposed to "There is" in English.

There are three bananas on the table.

Hay tres plátanos en la mesa.

We needed to discuss the usage and implementation of *haber* because that brings us into our next lesson.

Lesson nine: A few more tenses...

I don't think that it would be particularly worthwhile in the scope of a beginner's book intended for people absolutely new to Spanish and perhaps even language learning in general for me to go through every single tense that you might use. My entire goal with this book at large is to get you to understand the underlying grammatical concepts so that you might actually be able to build on them through proper experimentation as well as through constantly trying out new things with the language.

However, there are two more tenses we're going to cover, both of them in the past tense. The reason we're not covering future tense is that for near future verbs, Spanish generally just uses the present tense anyhow, often alongside a time marker. The other Spanish future tense is meant for dates and events which are farther off, and in my opinion as somebody who writes about and works with languages, I don't think that's a particularly paramount subject for new learnings and I don't realistically see time spent on that tense to be worthwhile as a beginner.

What I will talk about however, is the *preterite* and the *perfect tense*.

The preterite is the tense which is used for events which are over and done with; things which happened once already and weren't continuous. This is the one that you need to focus on, and for a very simple reason: you very well may start off a conversation with the fact that you don't speak Spanish particularly well. And if you *were* to do that, you likely wouldn't even need the perfect tense at all. It's not likely or common for introductory Spanish speakers to feel the need to express themselves in the past tense in exclusive or esoteric ways.

If you need to form the preterite with an *-ar* verb, all you have to do is drop the -ar and append the following endings: -é, -aste, -ó, -amos, and -aron.

Here is the *-ar* preterite conjugated for the verb *enviar*.

Enviar - *to send (preterite)*

Conjugation	Meaning	Pronunciation
Yo *envié.*	I sent.	yoh ehn-vee-ey
Tú *enviaste.*	You sent.	too ehn-vee-ahs-tay
Él/ella/usted *envió.*	He/she/you sent.	el/ey-yah/oos-ted ehn-vee-oh
Nosotros *enviamos.*	We sent.	noh-soh-tros enviamos
Ellos/Ellas/Ustedes *enviaron.*	They/they/you all sent.	ey-yohs/ey-yahs/oos-ted-ehs ehn-vee-ah-rohn

Likewise, to form it for an *-er* or *-ir* verb, you just drop the ending and tack on either *-í, -iste, -ió, -imos,* or *-ieron.* Let's try this out really quickly by using the verb *vivir*.

Vivir - *to live (preterite)*

Conjugation	Meaning	Pronunciation
Yo *viví.*	I lived.	yoh vee-vee
Tú *viviste.*	You lived.	too vee-vees-tey.
Él/ella/usted *vivió.*	He/she/you lived.	el/ey-yah/oos-ted vee-vee-oh
Nosotros *vivimos.*	We lived.	noh-soh-tros vee-vee-mohs
Ellos/Ellas/Ustedes *vivieron.*	They/they/you all lived.	ey-yohs/ey-yahs/oos-ted-ehs vee-vee-ehr-ohn

The present perfect tense is very easy. All that you need is the verb *haber* and the verb you'd like to form into the present perfect.

The present perfect carries the same weight as saying something like "I have cooked" or "She has laughed" in English. It's not always a 1 to 1 correlation, but there are a lot of times where the situational usage will certainly match up. And what's more is that forming past participles is absurdly easy in Spanish for regular verbs. All that you do is drop the *-ar*, *-er*, or *-ir* ending and replace it, either with *-ado* for *-ar* verbs or *-ido* for *-ir* or *-er* verbs.

So if we were to take the verb *vivir* again, we could say "I have lived" in the present perfect tense like so:

(Yo) he vivido.

It's a really simple lesson to take home, but it's an important tense to understand nonetheless.

Lesson ten: one last thing...

In case you didn't know, you obviously can negate things in Spanish. You do so by simply adding *no* before the verb:

Como carne.

No como carne.

The first sentence means "I eat meat", and the second means "I don't eat meat". It's a simple lesson, but infinitely important nonetheless.

Chapter 2: Pronunciation

I'm going to be straightforward as I say this: as a Spanish learner, you have it easy. Spanish has ridiculously easy pronunciation compared to other languages. It makes up for it with difficulty in other areas and a bizarre amount of esotericism compared to other major Romance languages (largely due to Arab influence). However, Spanish pronunciation is simple and predictable. You're hardly going to have a problem with any of it going forward.

The first thing that we need to talk about is the basic vowel sounds. Coming from English, it's really easy to pronounce things like you would in English, especially if it resembles an English word that you know. However, you can't do this. Spanish vowels are absolutely finite in their pronunciation and not saying them correctly is the fast track to sounding like an absolutely inexperienced Spanish speaker.

Here are the vowel sounds for Spanish, alongside how they're pronounced.

a will sound much like the first O in *October*.
e will sound like the *ay* in the word *bay* if the syllable ends in a vowel. If it ends in a consonant, then it will sound like the *e* in *net*.
i will sound like the *ee* in *tree*.
o will sound like the *o* in *rope* if the syllable ends in a vowel. If it ends in a consonant, it will sound like *o* in the word *hot*.
u will sound like the *oo* in *school*, unless it's in any of the following letter groups: gue, gui, qu. In these cases, it will be silent.
y will sound like the Spanish *i* when it is used as a vowel.

And naturally, Spanish has diphthongs as well. Diphthongs are the resultant sound of two vowels being put together. Generally, in Spanish at least, they're just the end result of the vowels being put together, and you can guess their sound just by putting the two appropriate vowel sounds together rather fast. Here are some common diphthongs regardless, and some familiar sounds you can associate with them:

ai will sound like the *i* in *bride*; **ay** will as well.
au will sound like the *ou* in *sound*.
ei will sound like the *ay* in *gray*; **ey** will as well.
eu will sound like the *ay-you* in *today-you*.
oi will sound like the *oy* in *coy;* **oy** will as well.
u before *any* vowel will sound like a *w*.
i before most vowels will sound like a *y;* **y** will as well.

Now it's time to move onto the consonant sounds. The consonant sounds will in certain places be very familiar, and if so, I'm not going to really bother expounding upon them. However, some are quite different, and so I'll go into detail on those.

B, if at the beginning of a word or when after a consonant, will sound like the English *b*. However, otherwise, it will sound like a mixture between an English *b* and an English *v*. **V** follows the same exact rules.

C, when it's before either a consonant or the vowels *a, u,* or *o,* will have a hard C sound like in "construction". Before the vowels *e* or *i*, however, the **C** will sound like an English *s*.

Ch always sounds the same: like the *ch* in *champion*. The reason I list this as it's own letter is twofold: firstly, English has both a *ch* and an *sh* sound reserved for the *ch* grouping. In Spanish, this isn't the case. However, there's also the fact that throughout history, the *ch* in Spanish has been treated as its own letter, before D but after C. Many older Spanish dictionaries and Spanish-English dictionaries will have the *Ch* words as their own category.

D will always sound like the English *d*, unless it's between vowels or following the letter *l* or the letter *n*, in either case it will be pronounced like the *th* in *that*.

F sounds like the English *f*.

G sounds like an English *h* but with more power, if before an *e* or an *i*; if it's before anything else, it sounds like the *g* in *gather*.

H is silent.

J sounds like an English *h* but with more power, and is silent whenever it is the last letter in a word.

K sounds like an English *k*.

L sounds like an English *l*.

Ll sounds like an English *y*, though it in some dialects has a slight *sh* sound to it. Pay attention to how the people around you pronounce it and mimic it, but use the *y* sound firstly.

M sounds like an English *m*.

N sounds like an English *n* in every instance except for when it precedes the letter *v*. In this case, it will sound like an English *m*.

Ñ sounds like an *ny* sound, as in *onion* or *bunion*.

P sounds like an English *p*.

Q is *always* followed by *u*, and the pair will *always* sound like an English *k*.

R is performed by way of an alveolar flap in the middle of a word, meaning a very soft touching of the tongue to the roof of the mouth. At the beginning of a given word or when it's following either the letter *l*, the letter *n*, or the letter *s*, it will have a powerful trill. At the end of a word, it has next to no trill, but still a small amount.

Rr indicates a very strong trill.

S will sound like an English *s* unless it's preceding either *b, d, g, l, m,* or *n,* in which case it will sound like an English *z*.

T will sound like an English *t*.

W will nearly always have a *v* sound. There are various linguistic reasons for this phenomenon, but I'm not going to go into them right here.

X sounds like an English *x* is between vowels, but before a given consonant it will sound like an English *s*. This is presuming the word isn't of Native or Aboriginal influence. If so, then it will sound like an *h*. (*Mexico* would sound like *Mey-hee-coh*, and *Texas* would sound like *Tey-hahs*.)

Y sounds like an English *y*.

Z generally just sounds like an English *z*.

As you can see, for the most part, Spanish pronunciation is generally very uniform. When there is a variation, change, or exception, it's likewise generally very easy to understand within the context of the language.

It's also worth noting the role of accent marks in Spanish. In the Spanish language, accent marks indicate *syllable stress* or serve to differentiate one word's spelling from another. This can be of grave importance, as some words without proper accents being written will take on totally different meanings which may at times even be personally embarrassing.

If you see an accent mark while reading Spanish, then it always means that you need to be certain that the syllable with the accent mark is getting quite a bit of stress and is enunciated *loudly* and *clearly*.

You are halfway done!

Congratulations on making it to the halfway point of the journey. Many try and give up long before even getting to this point, so you are to be congratulated on this. You have shown that you are serious about getting better every day. I am also serious about improving my life, and helping others get better along the way. To do this I need your feedback. Click on the link below and take a moment to let me know how this book has helped you. If you feel there is something missing or something you would like to see differently, I would love to know about it. I want to ensure that as you and I improve, this book continues to improve as well. Thank you for taking the time to ensure that we are all getting the most from each other.

Chapter 3: Basic Conversation

I'd be doing you a major disservice if I didn't teach you the very basics of Spanish conversation. The reason I've held off to this point is because a lot of language courses will start off by giving you the basic phrases of a language. That's great for letting you say hello and goodbye to people, but when it comes to building statements with any sort of actual meat to them, it's an uphill battle because you don't actually know anything about the language yet.

For example, before you even picked up this book, you most likely at least knew the word *hola* from having heard it in any number of North American sources involving Spanish speakers. But how much does that matter for having genuine discussion with Spanish speakers? Does that knowledge of *hola* allow you in any capacity to walk up to a Spanish stranger and do anything but say "hello" to them?

The answer, of course, is no. That's an utterly ridiculous notion in most every possible conceivable way. That is thus the very reason that I've held off going over all of this up until now: it simply wasn't necessary and would get in the way of actually *understanding* Spanish in any sort of meaningful manner.

But now that you understand the pronunciation and a lot of basic verbiage, I feel as though we're at a reasonable point where I can give you introductions to conversation without making myself feel like I'm making the language seem like it's anything but what it is: a language, with a thriving set of verb conjugations and unique articles and all of these awesome features that extend far, far beyond "holá".

Anyhow, for the sake of this chapter, we're going to work through a number of phrases one at a time with a brief explanation of everything that we're doing.

The first thing that you do in any given conversation is *initiate* it. Well, this isn't necessarily always true - some people are very pragmatic and get right to the point. But for most people, saying salutations is just a normal part of any given conversation, or perhaps things which aren't even really conversation. Perhaps you're passing by somebody you know in the school or workplace and want to acknowledge them. That's another situation in which you'd find knowing salutations to be a great advantage.

Spanish has a great many salutations and the one that you use depends upon a number of variables, of course.

There's, of course, the general use *hola* (oh-la). This just means "hello" in English. The etymology of the word "hola" is deeply interesting, but it's of course beyond the scope of this book.

Anyhow, there are also the greetings which have to do with the time of day. There is *buenos días (bwey-nohs di-ahs)*. This means literally "good morning" and is one of the more common Spanish greetings aside from *hola*. There also is *buenas tardes (bwey-nahs tar-dehs)*, which means *good evening*. This isn't used as often as a conventional salutation, though it certainly can be used as one with no problem. The last one in this category is *buenas noches (bwey-nahs no-chess)*. This means literally "good night" and its usage is unwavering; you will almost never ever use this as a salutation. You generally will only use this as a goodbye to somebody for the night is you know that you won't be seeing them again that night.

Lastly, there is *muy buenos. (moy bwey-nohs)*. This is a very general greeting as compared to other ones such as *buenos días* and *hola*. You can use this greeting at pretty much any time of day without anybody batting an eye.

So after all of that, we're now officially in the conversation, engaging in the nigh professional art of small talk. These small talk sessions generally almost always start by asking somebody how they are or how they're doing. There are a ton of ways to ask this sort of question in Spanish.

Firstly, there are the more formal and boring routes to be taken. To simply ask "How are you?", you first need to think about who you're talking to. Are you speaking to somebody your age? Younger? Older? Have you met them before? Then you need to pick either the informal or the formal way to ask based upon your evaluations. The informal way to ask is to simply "*¿Cómo estas?*" (co-moh es-tahs), meaning in a literal sense "how are you?". The formal way is just the usted inversion of the prior question: *¿Cómo está usted? (co-moh es-ta oos-ted)*. This means the same thing as before, but this version is of course to be reserved for meeting new people or for talking to people who are in a position of superiority.

On top of that, there are more casual ways to ask. You could say "how's it going?": *¿Cómo te va?* (co-moh teh va)

Simply asking "what's up?" is certainly not out of the question: *¿Qué tal?* (kay tall)

Neither would be asking something along the lines of "what's happening?"- *¿Qué pasa?* (kay pah-sah) - or "How have you been?": *¿Cómo has ido?* (co-moh ahs ee-do)

All in all, there are a ton of ways to ask somebody exactly how they're doing in Spanish. There are likewise a huge number of ways in which you could respond to this very question. Note that being in a foreign country or situation means that the culture is inevitably different; in America and England, when we ask "how are you?", we do so as a courtesy and generally not in the seeking of a very well-thought out response or any sort of genuine emotional discourse.

Certain other countries aren't like this, and if you ask how they are, they'll tell you how they are.

But for all intents and purposes, you may or may not give a very deep response. Should you choose to go with a more "standard" response, there are a number of different ways in which you could phrase it.

You could start with the quintessential *bien, gracias* (byen, grah-see-as) which means simply "well/fine, thank you." You could also opt for "very well" by saying *muy bien* (moy byen). You could insert a certain amount of nihilistic apathy into your conversation by saying *Como siempre* which technically means "like always" but carries the weight more like "I am as I always seem to be." If you're not feeling well, you can say that you're sick by saying either *estoy enfermo* or *estoy enferma* depending upon your gender, men saying the first and women saying the second. And if you're not doing too well, you could say *más o menos* (moss oh men-ohs) meaning "so-so", or you could say *mal* which translates to simply "badly" or "poorly".

Then, there are multiple different ways in which you could say goodbye. There are a few generally used ones, and a few which are geared towards more special purposes.

The two general purpose ones that you need to know are *adiós* and *chao*. Both are common enough that I'm not going to tell you how to pronounce them. If you're on the up, you very well may notice a parallel between Spanish and neighboring Romance language Italian here, where *ciao* is used as a form of goodbye. Both of these are acceptable ways to say goodbye.

If you'll be seeing the person soon, you could tell them *Hasta pronto (ahs-tah pronto)*. But when I say *soon,* I mean **soon**. This is one place where the common conception of "soon" as used in the U.S. or Britain generally doesn't cut it in other timetables.

If you're just going to see them at a later point in time, you could say *Hasta luego (ahs-tah lwey-go)*. This could imply a lack of certainty about when you'll meet again, however. It, as many things do, ultimately depends upon the context in which it's used.

The last one we're going to talk about here is *Hasta la vista (ahs-tah lah vees-tah,* but honestly, who doesn't know how to pronounce this one thanks to Hollywood?). This phrase means essentially "Until next time" or "untill we meet again". This one too can communicate a lack of certainty dependent upon the context.

On top of all of that, there are some essential phrases that you have absolutely got to know in order to ask for help in Spanish, or otherwise get around.

Firstly, there are two forms of "excuse me" you need to know. The first, *perdón*, means "excuse me" in the sense of "excuse me, could I ask you about something?"

The other form of excuse me, *con permiso*, has a meaning more along the lines of "Please excuse me", when you're needing somebody to move out of your way.

You also need to know how to say thank you and sorry. In fact, more people need to know how to do this in their *native* language. The way that you say "thank you" in Spanish is straightforward: *Gracias*. Nearly everybody knows that term. And the way you say sorry is additionally simple: *Lo siento (lo syen-toh)*.

It's most certainly also worth you learning how to say *please* in Spanish because you invariably are going to need to at some point. You do so by saying *por favor. (pour fah-vor)*

And lastly, at some point, eventually you're going to have to ask for help in some way, shape, or form. The way to do this is by saying *necesito ayuda (ney-cess-ee-toh ah-you-dah)*. This means literally "I need help" or "I need aid". You'll also notice that this very simple phrase is built off of the verb *necesitar*, conjugated for the first person as worked with in chapter one.

There's a lot of things you'll need to learn before you're ready for the streets, but hopefully now, you've got a solid enough foundation you can at least be courteous.

Chapter 4: Pronouns Redux: Direct Object and Indirect Object

We spoke earlier in the book about the manifold uses of *subject pronouns* and how they're used in English in order to enrich our sentences and make them less monotonous or unwieldy, and how they're ditched almost entirely in Spanish after conjugating the verb due to their very verbose conjugation system.

It'd be a mortal sin for me to actually finish up this book and somehow leave out the idea of more advanced pronouns. You're going to inevitably end up needing to use these, and likely quite often. The manner by which we naturally speak English is absolutely littered with these things. They're peppered throughout essentially every sentence that we speak. The same manner of speaking applies to Spanish as well. Nobody on earth likes redundancy, and not having some kind of pronouns system in place not only endorses but *enforces* redundancy.

The first form of pronouns that we're going to focus on at this point in time are the *direct object pronouns*. Direct object pronouns are pronouns which stand in for the direct object of the sentence. In case you're unclear what a direct object is, it is the thing which takes the brunt of a verb or an action as indicated by the structure, context, and intention of the sentence.

I actually feel like before we jump into the *mechanics* of direct object pronouns, I should make the distinction between direct objects and indirect objects and why the distinction even really matters.

Direct objects are, as I said, objects which go along with the verb, whereas indirect objects are not. They are *affected* by the verb and the direct object, but they are in no way attached to them. The way that I like to say it is this: the sentiment of the sentence can completely and wholly exist even without the inclusion of the indirect object. It may be significantly vaguer, but the resultant thought is still a complete syntactically and grammatically correct sentence.

Take the following sentence for example:

I sent the card to her.

If we were to break this sentence down into its essential components, it would look as follows:

I - subject; indicates the person or thing which is actively undergoing the verb.

sent - verb; specifically a simple past verb which indicates that the person has already performed the given action.

the card - direct object; This is the thing which is being directly affected by the verb. Without the verb *send*, there is no *the card* in this statement; without the *the card*, there is nothing to be *sent* in this statement. You can test the veracity of this by trying to rewrite the sentence without the direct object. "I am sending."/"I send." Great. What is being sent exactly? Without a direct object, these sentences make no sense.

to her. - indirect object; This is the thing which is being indirectly affected by the verb and is the end recipient of the consequences of the action of the verb. That is to say that the *indirect* object is non-essential where the *direct* object is essential. If you're ever confused in a sentence as to which is which, the first thing you should do is look for a preposition - indirect objects are usually sitting after a "to" or "at". However, the other thing you can do is try to rewrite the sentence once for each object without including the other. (In your head, if you'd like - doing it in real life would be rather wasteful.) The one which makes the least sense is invariably the one wherein the direct object has been removed. Compare "I sent the card." to "I sent to her." The only times that the second structure are permissible are when it's an idiomatic structure wherein the direct object is heavily implied or otherwise unneeded (consider the Victorian-era idiomatic phrasal verb "to send for [somebody]" meaning "to summon [somebody]", which has its roots in sending somebody like a messenger to go and get the person in question).

In other words, you will know which is the direct object and which isn't by which one can be taken out without the sentence losing any and all practical meaning.

So how do we express these sorts of pronouns in English? Well, let's shift our focus to the direct object pronouns again.

The way that we express direct object pronouns are by the use of pronouns such as "*me*", "*it*", "*him*", "*them*", and so forth. Let's take that sentence again. "I sent the card to her." *Her* is a indirect object pronoun because it replaces the traditional indirect object of the sentence which would be the *person's name*.

This indeed also turns this into a discussion of when you would use direct objects; the answer is after establishing relevancy for them. If a person or thing is mentioned by you or somebody else in a sentence, and that becomes the subject of the conversation, then you can by all means start to use object pronouns as heavily as you wish. If you fail to have some sort of initial object concept presented either by you or somebody else, all you're going to do is sound a tad bit confused at best or a tad bit crazy at worst.

Pro

In English, if I wanted to make this sentence simpler though, I could. Relatively easily too. Since we say "I sent the card" instead of "a card", we can boldly assume that the topic of conversation has already been established to be about both the card and the girl in question. So we could simplify this by replacing "the card" with the relevant direct object pronoun which would here be "it". So the sentence could become "I sent it to her." Following so far?

Spanish treats this sort of thing in a rather simple way. The Spanish layout for verbs and objects is flipped though. Their format for this sort of thing is as follows:

(subject) (indirect object) (direct object) (verb)

This format is often referred to as *SIODOV*.

There are several different direct object pronouns in Spanish. Their general meaning is as such:

Direct Object Pronouns

Pronoun	Meaning
Me	Me
Te	You
Lo	Him or It depending upon context
La	Her or It depending upon context
Nos	Us
Os	You (plural)
Los/las	Them

And the indirect object pronouns are very similar. Their only real difference is the dropping of gender in the third person pronouns.

Indirect Object Pronouns

Pronoun	Meaning
Me	Me
Te	You
Le/se	Him, Her, or It depending upon context
Nos	Us

Os	You (plural)
Les/se	Them

So let's go back to our example sentence, "I sent the card to her." When we write this in Spanish, before taking into account the direct object, we're going to transform "to her" into an indirect object, like so:

*I sent the card **to her***.

*(Yo) **Le** envié la tarjeta.*

Yo is in parentheses because in virtually all forms of spoken and written Spanish, you'd drop the subject pronoun. If you didn't, then you'd risk sounding like you have no idea what you're saying and likewise have no business speaking Spanish in the first place.

Now, we can convert "la tarjeta" into a direct object pronoun so we're saying what is the Spanish equivalent of "I sent her it." or "I sent it to her." Super simple but pretty involving.

Since *la tarjeta* is a feminine noun, we need to use the third person singular feminine direct object pronoun. This would of course be *la*. And according to the presented rules of the *SIODOV* protocol, we're going to smush that in between our indirect object pronoun and our verb. So our sentence would come out like this:

(Yo) **le** la envié.

So we went from a massive and bulky sentence to something that's rather elegant. (Provided you have the appropriate context to make sense of a vague statement like "I sent her it" or "Le la envié.")

That draws this lesson on pronouns to an end, I'm afraid.

Conclusion

Thank for making it through to the end of *Learn Spanish: A Fast and Easy Guide for Beginners to Learn Conversational Spanish*, let's hope it was informative and able to provide you with all of the tools you need to achieve your goals whatever they may be.

The next step is to build upon the knowledge you've procured. As I'm sure you've noticed, my intent in this book wasn't to flood you over with vocabulary words or make you memorize a million things. Rather, my sole intent was that you walk away understanding the mechanical foundations of Spanish impeccably well.

The beauty of language is that it's the fundamental crux of civilization. There is no way that we could have developed anywhere near as far as we have had we not had the ability to communicate via spoken and written language. Truly, language is one of the most beautiful things in the universe.

That's why I feel so honored to have been afforded the opportunity to help you to understand Spanish better as you learn and go forward with it. My sincere hope is that I've given you at the very least a solid foundation that you can build *on top* of, because I know that my pet peeve with language learning books are those that fail to teach certain things in depth and are effectively trying to build a brick house on a very shaky foundation of linguistic knowledge.

And to be quite frank with you, I don't feel like that approach works, either. Only practice and immersion can make somebody a better language learner.

If at any point going forward with learning Spanish or French or Chinese or whatever that you may learn in the future, you feel that you're unable to full carry out your potential, or you feel that you just have hit a wall and can't go any further, then for me, quit lying to yourself. Absolutely anybody can learn another language. It takes time and work and dedication, often a lot more than most people have, but there are people born into bilingualism and trilingualism constantly. Not only that, but those same kids will often go on to learn yet *another* language later in life.

I guess the point that I'm trying to make here in closing is that my teaching method is a tad unorthodox because my whole belief in language learning is that giving you a long list of vocabulary words to memorize isn't the way to go about it; I genuinely feel that the only way for you to improve is through constant and concentrated effort being actively put forth towards a given language, and exerting energy in the general direction of making yourself better.

If you wish to flesh out your vocabulary, the way I earnestly recommend doing it is going to http://wordreference.com/enes/ and http://spanishdict.com/conjugate/ and working as hard as you can. Start writing a private blog or journal in order to learn new words and phraseologies. And, if you do find yourself wishing for more vocabulary-centric learning, I highly recommend Duolingo.

Finally, if you found this book useful in anyway, a review on Amazon is always appreciated!

Free membership into the Mastermind Self Development Group!

For a limited time, you can join the Mastermind Self Development Group for free! You will receive videos and articles from top authorities in self development as well as a special group only offers on new books and training programs. There will also be a monthly member only draw that gives you a chance to win any book from your Kindle wish list!

If you sign up through this link http://www.mastermindselfdevelopment.com/specialreport you will also get a special free report on the Wheel of Life. This report will give you a visual look at your current life and then take you through a series of exercises that will help you plan what your perfect life looks like. The workbook does not end there; we then take you through a process to help you plan how to achieve that perfect life. The process is very powerful and has the potential to change your life forever. Join the group now and start to change your life!
http://www.mastermindselfdevelopment.com/specialreport

Help me improve this book

While I have never met you, if you made it through this book I know that you are the kind of person that is wanting to get better and is willing to take on tough feedback to get to that point. You and I are cut from the same cloth in that respect. I am always looking to get better and I wish to not just improve myself, but also this book. If you have positive feedback, please take the time to leave a review. It will help other find this book and it can help change a life in the same way that it changed yours. If you have constructive feedback, please also leave a review. It will help me better understand what you, the reader, need to make significant improvements in your life. I will take your feedback and use it to improve this book so that it can become more powerful and beneficial to all those who encounter it.

You will also love these other great titles from Mastermind Self Development!

You will want to check out these other great titles Mastermind Self Development. All available in the Kindle store or you can just click on covers below.

http://mybook.to/positive

http://viewbook.at/veganbook

You can also find these titles by searching them in the Kindle store on Amazon.

Learn Spanish

Short Stories for Beginners to Learn Spanish Fast and Easy

Free membership into the Mastermind Self Development Group!

For a limited time, you can join the Mastermind Self Development Group for free! You will receive videos and articles from top authorities in self development as well as a special group only offers on new books and training programs. There will also be a monthly member only draw that gives you a chance to win any book from your Kindle wish list!

If you sign up through this link http://www.mastermindselfdevelopment.com/specialreport you will also get a special free report on the Wheel of Life. This report will give you a visual look at your current life and then take you through a series of exercises that will help you plan what your perfect life looks like. The workbook does not end there; we then take you through a process to help you plan how to achieve that perfect life. The process is very powerful and has the potential to change your life forever. Join the group now and start to change your life!
http://www.mastermindselfdevelopment.com/specialreport

Table of Contents

Introduction

Congratulations on downloading *Learn Spanish: Short Stories for Beginners to Learn Spanish Fast and Easy* and thank you for doing so.

There are a lot of reasons that you may want to learn Spanish. Maybe you're going on vacation to Latin America or to Spain and you're wanting to have a solid grasp on the vocabulary before you go. Maybe you're just wanting to learn for your own sake, so that you can further yourself as a person. Maybe you're wanting to pad your resume a bit. Maybe you're doing it so your career prospects are better. One way or another, the point is that you're wanting to learn Spanish, and you're wanting to learn it *fast*. Well, in that case, this book is just the one for you.

The intent of this book is simple: we're going to start from next to nothing in terms of Spanish and then slowly become more and more engrossed in the language. You'll go from an absolute beginner to relatively proficient in no time at all.

In the meantime, we're going to showcase a lot of different features of Spanish that you'll need to know to be a competent speaker, including verb tenses and conjugation, as well as little notes about usage and so forth.

This book is going to follow the adventures of a young girl named Maria and her exciting family as we go forward trying to understand the basics of this beautiful language. We're going to meet them and follow them as they tell us about themselves and go on a couple different adventures.

There are plenty of books on this subject on the market, thanks again for choosing this one! Every effort was made to ensure it is full of as much useful information as possible, please enjoy!

Chapter 1: A Note on Language Learning

I'm assuming by the nature of this book that it may be your first foray into language learning. As such, I felt that it was appropriate for me to take some time to explain some things about language learning in general, as well as the Spanish language in particular. Don't worry, this won't take a long time, all it is is a collection of observations and grammatical/linguistic notes that I've made about language learning and Spanish itself.

The first thing that I always hear from people trying to learn a new language is that it's overwhelmingly difficult, or that they're simply not cut out for it for this reason or that. That's essentially a total lie. Anybody can learn languages. Our brains are hardwired for language.

Allow me to put it this way: what other animal communicates through language as complex as ours? We are as social of an animal as ants, bees, or dogs, all of which have complex systems of communication for speaking to one another, yet none of them are still as complicated as ours. For this reason, we can surmise that not only do we *have* the ability to speak, but we are meant to *use* the ability to speak. Not necessarily in a divine sense but in the sense that it's an evolutionary trait, an advantage that we've developed to give us an edge on the rest of the animal kingdom. And indeed, it has! This particular little aspect of humanity has allowed us to go from nomadic plains dwellers to bustling metropoli. In other words, language deserves ample respect; however, so does one's ability to *learn* language.

So maybe that's why you're reading this book. Maybe traditional approaches to language learning have really burned you out and you're looking for something a tad more interactive. Well, let me tell you that you're without a doubt making the right first steps.

People who can speak multiple languages are known as *polyglots*. Some are simply savants, some are hobbyists, and some are born or groomed into situations where they need to speak multiple different languages. Regardless of the reason, most polyglots will agree that the single best way to learn a language is through the concept of immersion. Why? Let me explain.

Back in the olden days, we had to attach words to *concepts*. For example, when you look at a *tree*, the tree isn't actually *finitely a tree*. It's simply a part of being that we have *called* a tree. However, a Spanish speaker would call it an *arból*, and a French speaker would call it an *arbre*. So, the tree isn't really a "tree" in any sense, it's just there, and you happen to call it a tree.

This is a key part of human development, recognizing these concepts. For example, before speech developed, we still had to recognize what was water, what was food, what was fire, and so forth. Failing to be able to recognize these concepts, even without a *name* for them, meant that we simply wouldn't survive.

Now fast forward a bit - language has developed, speech has developed, there are suddenly names for these concepts. Being able to communicate *about* these concepts - asking where water is, for example, or if you could use a stone ax for just a moment - could make a world of difference. So, just like our brain is tuned to recognize concepts, our brain is tuned to attach these concepts to words and sounds.

The idea of immersion is simply the notion of tapping into that part of your brain that connects these sounds to words. That's an easy enough concept, right? This book is a crash course in immersion.

Every chapter is going to start out with a story in Spanish. That is going to be followed by the same story in English, for comparison. Afterwards, we're going to be picking out key parts of the Spanish story - just enough that you can fill in the blanks on the other parts, the way your brain is *supposed* to learn language.

However, in its incredibly varied 1.5 million years of development, language and speech have, believe it or not, diverged into several different paths. What this means, primarily, is that every language has its own unique features that set it apart from other languages. The exact number and depth of these features depends upon the languages you're comparing. For example, languages can be grouped into *families* that developed alongside one another or share multiple cultural and/or linguistic similarities. Spanish, French, and Italian are all members of the *Romance* language family. This means that even though they have different vocabularies, they derive from the same region and developed along similar lines and so will share many similarities, too. These languages can be broken down even *further* into very specific categories, but for right now that's all you need to know.

The reason I'm telling you this is because English and Spanish are, unfortunately, *not* from the same language family. English is a Germanic language, descending from the West Germanic languages. However, the fact that the United Kingdom is extremely close to both Spain and France and the heavy involvement of the Normans in England in the Middle Ages, there are quite a few similarities. These are mainly in the way of vocabulary. For the most part, English grammar is very specifically Germanic and not Romantic.

So, what's the difference? Well, there are a few things that you're going to have to get used to if you want to be an adept Spanish speaker (or an adept speaker of any Romance language, for that matter!).

One of the first of these concepts is verb conjugation. Fortunately for us (or unfortunately, depending on how you look at it), English doesn't have a very significantly difficult conjugation system. In fact, it has one of the *easiest*. For English verbs, you either just keep the verb as is, or you add an *s* to it. (For the present tense, at least.)

Then for the future tense, all you do is add an auxiliary verb - "will" or "am going to". If it's in the very near future ("I'm playing music tonight") then you don't even add an auxiliary verb! So, what about past tense? That's simple too, you either just add *-ing* and the verb *was* ("I was walking") or just an *-ed* to the end of the word. ("I jumped!")

Overall, verbs in English are extremely easy.

Well, this isn't quite the truth in Spanish. Romance language verbs are normally heavily conjugated. What this means is that they have the ending changed to correspond to the specific *person* (first, second, or third-person) and *number of people* (singular, plural). To that end, verbs in Spanish are constantly changing, far more than they are in English.

For example, take the verb "*to eat*" in English. If we were to say this in English, we would conjugate it like so:

> *I eat.*
> *You eat.*
> *He/she/it eats.*
> *We eat.*
> *You all eat.*
> *They eat.*

And that's all. In Spanish, it's rather different. The verb for "to eat" in Spanish is *comer*, and it would conjugate like so:

> *Yo como.*
> *Tu comes.*
> *Él/ella/usted come.*
> *Nosotros comemos.*
> *Ellos/ellas/ustedes venden.*

(*Ustedes* in Spanish means "you all". In Castilian Spanish - the Spanish spoken in Spain - the term *vosotros* is used. However, since this book focuses upon Latin American Spanish, *vosotros* will be left out. If you do need to learn *vosotros*, it's extremely easy to build up from the starting point that I'm giving you.)

And that's just the present tense. That's not even accounting for the various other tenses! What's more is that as English speakers, a lot of things regarding verb tenses come very naturally to us, to the point that we don't ever really even think about them. The reality is that the little things about verb tenses make a lot of differences. For example, there's a huge difference in French between the passé composé and the imparfait, and swapping one for the other can change the entire meaning of the sentence. Not to mention decide whether a sentence is semantically correct!

I'll quit going on about verbs now. You also need to be aware of articles and nouns before you move on to the next part of the book, because they function differently than English.

See, many languages have a concept of "grammatical gender". This doesn't mean that the noun is literally either a male or a female. (Or, in the case of some languages, a neuter!) In fact, the grammatical concept of gender has very little to do with sexual gender at all. After all, how arbitrary would that be? Tables and apples can't be females in any finite sense, just as bananas can't be male in any finite sense. So why is the *noun* for these words one gender or another?

There is quite a vivid explanation for this one. It goes back to linguistic development. However, I'm not going to bore you with the raw details of how one language becomes what it has become. That's not very relevant to the book. The key thing to remember is the idea of *sound harmony*. Across languages, words have always needed to sound "correct" in one sense or another. This meant that certain sounds would match to one another in order to make a far prettier language. These sounds can sometimes be a bit arbitrary, but generally they're easy to follow. For example, in Spanish, generally if a noun ends in an -*o* then it will be a masculine noun. Generally, if a noun ends in an -*a* then it will be a feminine noun. But, as there are a great many nouns with a great number of different endings, it can be a little bit of a cluster in order to actually remember what sounds correlate to what gender generally. This is something that will come to you with experience. Even for experienced speakers, it can be a little difficult and can lead to embarrassing mix-ups! For example, *la papa* means "the potato", but *el Papa* means "the pope". Imagine getting those two confused!

So where do the differences here actually come up? Well, one of the most evident places are in *articles*. Articles are the things which tell you *what* and *how many* of a noun is being mentioned. Consider the difference between "*the apple*" and "*an apple*". Now, consider the difference between "*an apple*" and "*some apples*". This is where articles really come in handy. They let you be specific in your referencing to the degree that you *need* to be in order to communicate effectively.

Spanish has two different types of articles: *indefinite* and *definite*. Definite articles will correlate to *the* and are simpler so we'll start with them.

Definite articles refer to a very specific instance of an object (or objects) that has been or is being referenced in an obvious manner. For example, "do you have *the* book?" is referencing a very *specific* and *definite* book.

The Spanish definite articles are categorized according to *gender* and *number*.

The singular masculine definite article is *el*.
The singular feminine definite article is *la*.
The plural masculine definite article is *los*.

The plural feminine definite article is *las*.

The Spanish *indefinite* articles correlate instead to "a", "an", or "some". Let's look at that sentence from earlier: "do you have *the* book?". If we were to use an indefinite article instead, it would be "do you have a book?", which is far vaguer than the one prior. Do you see what I'm getting at here? Choosing the right article can make the difference between being understood or not.

Now, those are the main grammatical concepts that you need to know before diving right into the book, so I thought it was worth going over them a bit. We will be tackling a few others as we go through the book, but I don't want to overwhelm you right from the get-go.

I should note that the pacing of this book may seem rather fast. However, please don't let that alarm you. This book is intended for at *least* two reads. The first read, you will likely not understand the stories much. That is what the English translations are for. The first read is to acquaint you with certain particular words and phrases in Spanish that are particularly important for you as a new Spanish speaker. The second (and beyond) read is for you to compare the texts that you now somewhat understand and see what you can piece together about the language that you didn't know before. Maybe you learn new words you didn't pick up the first time. (You almost certainly will!) Maybe you just slowly figure out how to phrase things in Spanish. One way or another, this book will seem like it has a steep learning curve. It does *not*. The book is very simple. You just have to be aware that it will take a few reads to fully understand everything that you are reading.

So, without further ado, let's jump in and introduce our characters for these stories!

Chapter 2: *¡Hola, Maria!* / Hello, Maria!

In Spanish

"**¡Hola!** Mi nombre es Maria. **¿Cómo estás? Tengo 12 años.** Tengo el pelo marrón y los ojos marrones. Tengo dos hermanos, Oscar y José. Oscar tiene 14 años y José tiene 16 años. Vivo con Oscar, José, y mis padres. Vivimos en El Paso, Texas. **Mis padres son de El Salvador**, sin embargo. Hablan mucho de El Salvador. Creo que lo echan de menos. Dicen que la vida en América es mucho mejor, sin embargo.

Voy a la escuela todos los días. Después de la escuela es cuando la diversión sucede. Cuando llego a casa de la escuela, tengo muchas cosas que me gusta hacer. Los martes, tengo una lección de piano a las 4 pm. En otros días, me gusta ver la televisión y leer libros. Lo que realmente me encanta es cantar, sin embargo. Quiero ser cantante cuando crezca. Mi cantante preferida es probablemente Ariana Grande. Ella me inspira.

Mis hermanos **también** son geniales. Oscar le encanta el fútbol. A pesar de que sólo tiene 14 años, sigue siendo muy bueno en ello. ¡Puede correr más rápido que nadie, y puede hacer un gol desde el centro del campo!

Mi otro hermano José le gustan las computadoras. Creo que quiere ser ingeniero. Papá está muy orgulloso de José, porque hace buenas notas. A pesar de que **papá** y **mamá** no ganan mucho dinero, siguen comprando a José sus cosas de computadora porque le encantan las computadoras tanto. Todos realmente pensamos que él puede hacer algo.

Tenemos un perro. Su nombre es Ringo. Él **le gusta** jugar. ¡Mastica todo! Todavía es muy joven.

Hay muchas familias como la nuestra, pero la mía es mi favorita. Todo el mundo es juguetón entre sí y agradable todo el tiempo. Mis hermanos me llaman Ratón porque tengo una pequeña nariz. No me importa, me hace reír.

De todos modos, **encantado de conocerle! ¡Adiós!**"

Ese era María, y estaba muy feliz de conocerle. Las siguientes historias van a seguir a María y su familia mientras hacen cosas alrededor de la ciudad. Este capítulo tuvo dos propósitos: familiarizarse con los verbos de tiempo presente y acostumbrarse a la lectura en español. Usted probablemente notó que mucho de lo que parece Inglés. Esto se debe a que las lenguas comparten palabras y han tenido un impacto entre sí a lo largo de los años.

Ese es el primer capítulo abajo. Es también el más corto. Sin embargo, era sólo una introducción! Ahora puedes ver a la familia de María mientras van y hacen cosas diferentes, y aprenden un lenguaje hermoso al mismo tiempo.

¡Buena suerte!

In English

"Hi! My name is Maria. How are you? I'm 12 years old. I have brown hair and brown eyes. I have two brothers, Oscar and José. Oscar is 14 and José is 16. I live with Oscar, José, and my mom and dad. We live in El Paso, Texas. My mom and dad are from El Salvador, though. They talk about El Salvador a lot. I think they miss it. They say that life in America is much better, though.

I go to school every day. After school is when the fun happens. When I get home from school, I have a lot of things I like to do. On Tuesdays, I have a piano lesson at 4 P.M. On other days, I like to watch television and read books. What I really love is to sing, though. I want to be a singer when I grow up. My favorite singer is probably Ariana Grande. She inspires me.

My brothers are cool, too. Oscar loves soccer. Even though he's only 14, he's still very good at it. He can run faster than anybody else, and can make a goal from the middle of the field!

My other brother José really likes computers. I think that he wants to be an engineer when he grows up. Daddy is really proud of José, because he makes good grades. Even though dad and mom don't make a lot of money, they still buy José his computer stuff because he loves computers so much. We all really think that he can do something with it.

We have a dog. His name is Ringo. He likes to play. He chews on everything! He's still very young, though.

There are a lot of families like ours, but mine is my favorite. Everyone is playful with each other and nice all the time. My brothers call me Mouse because I've got a small nose. I don't mind though, it makes me laugh.

Anyway, it's nice to meet you! Goodbye!"

That was Maria, and she was really happy to get to know you. The next few stories are going to follow Maria and her family as they do things around the town. This chapter served two purposes: to get you acquainted with *present tense verbs* and to get you used to reading in Spanish. You probably noticed that a lot of it looks like English. That's because the languages share words and have had an impact on each other over the years.

That's the first chapter down. It's also the shortest. However, it was only an introduction! Now you get to see Maria's family as they go and do different things, and learn a beautiful language at the same time.

Good luck!

Grammar Notes/Vocab

As you can see, there were a fair amount of different vocabulary words that we needed to cover in this chapter. However, as I also promised, I'm not overloading you with things you need to know *right this minute*. As you make your way through this gorgeous language, you'll find that you pick quite a bit up on your own. The language is actually incredibly intuitive and easy to pick up once you understand the core concepts behind it. Perhaps that's the reason that so many people around the globe speak it with little to no issue!

Before we get into the vocabulary, there's one thing we really need to talk about: *pronouns*.

There are a few different types of pronouns in Spanish, but for right now, we're going to talk about *subject pronouns* and *object pronouns* in vague terms. Subject pronouns are those which refer to the person that is the *subject* of the sentence.

For example, in the sentence "I will throw it to him.", *I* is the subject, as *I* is the one carrying out the action.

In the first chapter, I briefly outlined these, but I'm going to expound upon these now a bit.

Spanish has several different subject pronouns - here they are, and the words they correlate to.

Yo - I

Tú - You

Él - He/it (masculine)

Ella - She/it (feminine)

Usted - You (formal)

Nosotros - We

Ellos - They (masculine/mixed)

Ellas - They (feminine)

Ustedes - You all/you guys

As you can see, they're relatively simple and we've already gone over them a bit.

Note, too, that since verb conjugation is so complex in Spanish and directs back to whoever the subject is, the subject will generally be dropped entirely in the sentence. So "Yo como" (I eat) becomes simply "Como".

The really tricky ones are *object pronouns*. There are two different types of objects: *direct objects* and *indirect objects*. Direct objects are the things which are directly affected by an action or a verb. Indirect objects are the thing which are indirectly affected by an action or a verb. A simpler way to put this is that you can *remove* the indirect object from a sentence and the verb-object phrase will still make sense.

"I throw the ball to him."

To him is the indirect object - "I throw the ball" still makes sense. "I throw to him" does *not*. It could informally, but only because the "it" (as in "I throw *it* to him") is implicit and doesn't need to be stated.

This brings us to the next point beyond distinguishing them: *direct* and *indirect object pronouns*.

Sometimes, a person will be the direct object. Like "I defeated *him*": *him* is the direct object. "I love *you*": *you* is the direct object. So, to account for this, we need multiple direct object pronouns.

In Spanish, the object pronouns go before the verb.

Let's take the phrase "I love you". In Spanish, you conjugate the verb: I love is *yo amo*.

We can drop the subject pronoun, so now it's just *amo*. But the *you* part is still missing. What can we do about that?

Well, we need to *add* a "you"!

These are the direct object pronouns in Spanish:

First-person singular: *me*

Second-person singular: *te*

Third-person singular: *lo/la*

First-person plural: *nos*

Second-person plural: *os*

Third-person plural: *los/las*

So, we'd need the *second person singular direct object pronoun*: *te*. If we put it before our verb, our sentence becomes "te amo"!

Here are the indirect object pronouns, largely similar:

First-person singular: *me*

Second-person singular: *te*

Third-person singular: *le*

First-person plural: *nos*

Second-person plural: *os*

Third-person plural: *les*

If you need both a *direct* and *indirect* object pronoun in the same sentence, your sentence follows the SIODOV order: *subject, indirect object, direct object, verb*. Remember SIODOV and you'll be in good shape!

The vocabulary for this chapter is as follows:

hola   -   *Hello!*

cómo estas? -   *How are you?* (informal)

Cómo está usted? -   *How are you?* (formal)

[ser] de (location)-   *am/is/are from*

también   -   *also*

papá/mamá -   *Mother/father (affectionate)*

se gusta   -   *to like (reflexive verb)*

encantado de

  concerle   -   *Pleased to meet you!*

adiós   -   Goodbye!

buena suerte   -   Good luck!

Verbs to learn are *ser*, *estar*, and *tener*. *Ser* and *estar* both mean "to be". The difference between them can be tricky at first. Generally, just remember - "how you feel and where you are, that is when you use *estar*"! *Estar* is for temporary states of being while *ser* is for more permanent qualities.

Ser

yo	soy
tú	eres
él/ella/usted	es
nosotros	somos
ellos/ellas/ustedes	son

Estar

yo	estoy
tú	estas
él/ella/usted	está
nosotros	estamos
ellos/ellas/ustedes	están

Tener

yo	*tengo*
tú	*tienes*

él/ella/usted	*tiene*
nosotros	*tenemos*
ellos/ellas/ustedes	*tienen*

You are halfway done!

Congratulations on making it to the halfway point of the journey. Many try and give up long before even getting to this point, so you are to be congratulated on this. You have shown that you are serious about getting better every day. I am also serious about improving my life, and helping others get better along the way. To do this I need your feedback. Click on the link below and take a moment to let me know how this book has helped you. If you feel there is something missing or something you would like to see differently, I would love to know about it. I want to ensure that as you and I improve, this book continues to improve as well. Thank you for taking the time to ensure that we are all getting the most from each other.

Chapter 3: *Un Día al Parque* / A Day at the Park

In Spanish

Es un día **soleado**. María y sus hermanos están en la habitación de José.

"Es un día tan bonito, ¿por qué estamos dentro?," dice Oscar.

"¡Porque no tengo gas para conducirnos a ninguna parte!" dice José.

"Estoy seguro de que si le preguntamos, mamá y papá nos llevaría a algún lugar," dice Oscar.

"¿Cómo dónde?" Dice José.

"¿Por qué no vamos todos al zoológico?," dice Oscar.

A María no le gusta eso. Ella piensa que los parques zoológicos son aburridos.

"Cuando vamos al zoológico, nos quedamos de pie. El zoológico aquí no es bueno!," dice María.

"¿Qué quieres hacer entonces, María?," dice José.

Maria piensa por un segundo.

"No estoy segura," dice finalmente María.

"Podríamos ir al parque," dice Oscar.

"¿Cuál?," dice María.

"¿Qué pasa con los karts y el minigolf?," dice José.

A Maria le gustaba el sonido de eso. Cuando va al parque con Oscar y José, siempre juegan sin ella. Ella es una muchacha de 12 años contra dos muchachos mayores así que la mayoría de los juegos de los deportes no son justos. Debido a esto, cuando van al parque ella normalmente no se divierte. Sin embargo, si hay go-karts y mini-golf, tal vez le gustará! ¡De hecho, ella puede incluso ganar!

"¡Creo que eso suena divertido!," dice María.

"Está bien, voy a pedirle a mamá ya papá que nos lleven," dice José.

José sale de la habitación y baja las escaleras para hablar con su mamá y papá. Mientras él se fue, Oscar y María miran una película en la televisión.

Pasa un minuto y luego José vuelve.

"¡Pueden llevarnos al parque!," dice José. Oscar y María sonríen. Todo el mundo va a sus habitaciones para prepararse para el parque. María se pone una camisa rosa y pantalones cortos azules. Oscar se pone una camisa verde y pantalones cortos negros. José decide usar una camisa naranja con pantalones cortos blancos. Todos usan zapatos blancos.

Oscar, María y José bajan. Dicen hola a su mamá y papá.

"¿Están todos listos?," dice el padre.

Todo el mundo dice que sí. Todos salen y suben al auto.

María no puede esperar a jugar al mini-golf.

"¡Vaya más rápido!", Le dice María a su padre.

"¡Voy tan rápido como puedo!" Dice su padre. Su madre se ríe.

La **ciudad** de El Paso es muy bonita en un hermoso día como este. El sol es muy **brillante**. El **cielo** es muy **azul**. ¡Todo parece perfecto! No hay una nube en el cielo. Porque es tan bonito, hay mucho tráfico. Todo el mundo está tratando de salir y disfrutar del día nublado! No es de extrañar.

Pronto llegan al parque. La madre y el padre deciden disfrutar del bonito día.

"Vamos al estanque para alimentar patos y sentarnos en el banco," dice el padre.

María se ríe. ¡Qué edad tienen sus padres! Ella está emocionada de hacer cosas. Cosas como mini-golf!

"¿Podemos ir a jugar al mini-golf ahora mismo? ¡Ahora mismo!," dice María.

"Claro, podemos hacer eso primero," dice José.

José, María y Oscar caminan a la parte del minigolf del parque. Ellos compran un juego de mini-golf. A continuación, obtener sus bolas y palos. A partir de aquí, pueden empezar! Ellos van al primer hoyo.

"¡Voy a golpearte!" dice María a los dos hermanos.

"¡No lo creo!," dice José.
El juego continúa. Un agujero tras otro, lentamente hacen su camino hasta el final del curso. María está feliz porque es un juego donde puede mantenerse al día con sus hermanos. Con la mayoría de los deportes sería difícil, porque ella es

mucho más pequeña. Con mini-golf, es más nivel.

Es tan nivel, de hecho, que cuando terminan el noveno hoyo, María gana después de todo! Ella empieza a regocijarse con sus dos hermanos. "¿Viste eso? ¡Gané! ," dice María.

"A nadie le gusta un ganador dolorido," dice Oscar.

"Muy bien, niños, cálmate!" Dice José. -¿Vamos a los karts ahora?

"Sí, quiero vencer a Oscar de nuevo!," dice María.

"¡Cállate!," dice Oscar.

"María, karts no es una carrera. No estás golpeando a nadie. ¡Solo estás tratando de divertirte e ir tan rápido como puedas! ," dice José.

"Eso suena menos divertido que derrotar a Oscar," dice María.

"Te divertirás. Vamos! ," dice José.

Todos caminan hasta el edificio de kart. Frente al edificio de karting es una pista realmente grande donde ya hay gente que compite con. María se pone nerviosa. ¡Van tan rápido!

Los tres niños caminan hasta el vendedor de carro. "Hola, necesitamos tres carros por favor".

-¿Qué edad tiene? -pregunta el vendedor, señalando a María.

"Tiene 12 años," dice José.

"Lo siento, tienes que tener 13 años para montar en un solo carro," dice el vendedor de carros.

María se pone triste. Ella puede estar nerviosa, pero eso no significa que no esté emocionada.

"Bueno, ¿puede viajar conmigo?," dice José.

"¿Qué edad tienes?", Pregunta el vendedor del carro.

"Tengo 16 años," dice.

"¿Tienes una licencia de conducir contigo?" Pregunta el vendedor del carro.

"Sí. Aquí tienes. "Agarra su cartera y saca su licencia.

La mujer lo mira. "Bueno. Necesito que firme esta renuncia.

"**Absolutamente**," dice José.

María se vuelve muy feliz otra vez. Ella consigue montar en un go-kart después de todo. Ella no puede esperar para acelerar alrededor de la pista y ver los árboles se convierten en un desenfoque a su alrededor!

"De acuerdo, ustedes son listos. Ir a la sala de espera. Ustedes dos estarán en el carro doble 14, y usted estará en el carro individual 3. "el vendedor del carro dice. Los niños hacen lo que se les dice. Ellos van a la sala de espera. Nunca ha sido tan difícil de esperar! Todos están impacientes por ponerse en la pista y empezar a conducir.

"¡Guau! Hace **calor**," dice Oscar.

-No será en un **segundo, hermano**. El viento y la velocidad te refrescan. "José responde.

"Eso no hace nada ahora mismo," dice Oscar.

"¡Deja de quejarte!," dice María. Ella golpea a su hermano en el brazo juguetonamente. Se ríe y ella también.

"Me quejo cuando quiero quejarme," dice Oscar.

"¡Lo veo!," dice María.

Finalmente, la línea comienza a moverse de nuevo. Las personas que estaban en la pista están regresando y tirando pulg El tipo en la línea de meta dice "Gracias, por favor, vuelva" a todo el mundo. María se pregunta si lo harán.

Cuando todo el que estaba en un carrito está fuera, otro hombre se levanta. Parece el hombre de la línea de meta. Ayuda a la gente a meterse en sus carros. Mira los sellos en las manos de los tres niños, y luego los lleva a sus carros.

María y José entran en su carro. José está en el volante. El hombre los abrocha, y tira más fuerte de María. "La seguridad en primer lugar!," dice. A continuación, gira la llave. El go-kart cobra vida.

El hombre de la línea de llegada recoge una señal. Dice "detener". Se detiene al lado de la pista. Cuando todos los karts están corriendo, dice: "En 3, puedes ir." ¡Entonces, él cuenta!

1 ...
2 ...

3!

María y José despegan. Van muy rápido. María no puede recordar si ella ha ido tan rápido antes! Ciertamente no lo cree. Hacen algunas vueltas y luego el paseo termina. El hombre que sostuvo la señal de stop ahora está sosteniendo un letrero que dice "Reduzca la velocidad, la vuelta final". José y María entran de nuevo en la sala de espera y esperan a que el hombre los suelte.

"¿Te divertiste?," dice José.

"¡Mucho!" dice María.

José sonríe porque sabe que ha hecho un buen trabajo como hermano. María también sonríe porque le gusta ir rápido.

Salen y se encuentran con Oscar.

"¿Qué tal, Oscar?" pregunta José.

"¡Súper divertido! Me alegro de haberlo hecho," dice Oscar.

"Yo también" dijo José. "¡Mamá y papá probablemente están preocupados! Vamos a encontrarlos."

Los tres van al estanque donde ven a su madre y su padre alimentando patos, como dijeron.

"¡Los patos son divertidos hoy!," dice el padre.

"Los patos siempre son divertidos, son patos," dice Oscar.

"¿Hay algo que quieran hacer los niños antes de irnos?," dice la madre.

María mira hacia el parque. "¿Podemos caminar el sendero?"

La madre sonríe. "Absolutamente."

La madre y el padre se levantan. María camina hacia el sendero y el resto sigue. María se ralentiza para que los demás puedan ponerse al día.

Caminan por el sendero y miran hacia el hermoso estanque también. Ellos piensan en lo perfecto que es el día, incluso si es un poco caliente. En el cielo, oyen a los pájaros cantar. Maria piensa en cómo quiere ser cantante. Su padre dice "que será usted!". María se ríe.

"¡Soy afortunado! Todos tenemos suerte," dice María.

“¿Por qué?” pregunta José.

“¡Porque la familia lo es todo!” responde María.

En este punto, terminan el rastro y caminan al coche. El padre los conduce a casa, y todos sonríen o duermen una siesta.

In English

It's a sunny day. Maria and her brothers are in José's room.

"It's such a pretty day, why are we inside?" Oscar says.

"Because I don't have gas to drive us anywhere!" José says.

"I'm sure that if we asked, mom and dad would take us somewhere." Oscar says.

"Like where?" José says.

"Why don't we all go to the zoo?" Oscar says.

Maria doesn't like that. She thinks zoos are boring.

"When we go to the zoo, we just stand around. The zoo here isn't any good!"
Maria says.

"What do you want to do then, Maria?" José says.

Maria thinks for a second.

"I'm not sure." Maria finally says.

"We could all go to the park!" Oscar says.

"Which one?" Maria says.

"What about the one with the go-karts and the mini golf?" José says.

Maria liked the sound of that. When she goes to the park with Oscar and José,
they always just play games without her. She's a 12-year-old girl against two older
boys so most sports games aren't fair. Because of this, when they go to the park
she normally doesn't enjoy herself. However, if there are go-karts and mini-golf,
maybe she will like it! In fact, maybe she can even win!

"I think that sounds fun!" Maria says.

"Okay, I'll go ask mom and dad to drive us." José says.

José leaves the room and goes downstairs to talk to his mom and dad. While he's
gone, Oscar and Maria watch a movie on the television.

A minute passes and then José comes back.

"They can drive us to the park!" José says. Oscar and Maria smile. Everyone goes to their rooms to get ready for the park. Maria puts on a pink shirt and blue shorts. Oscar puts on a green shirt and black shorts. José decides to wear an orange shirt with white shorts. They all wear white shoes.

Oscar, Maria, and José go downstairs. They say hello to their mom and dad.

"Is everybody ready?" the father says.

Everybody says yes. They all go outside and get into the car.

Maria can't wait to play mini-golf.

"Go faster!" Maria says to her father.

"I'm going as fast as I can!" her father says. Her mother laughs.

The city of El Paso is very pretty on a beautiful day like this. The sun is very bright. The sky is very blue. Everything seems perfect! There isn't a cloud in the sky. Because it's so pretty, there is a lot of traffic. Everybody is trying to get out and enjoy the cloudy day! No wonder.

Soon, they arrive at the park. The mother and father decide to enjoy the pretty day.

"We are going to the pond to feed ducks and to sit on the bench." the father says.

Maria laughs. How old her parents are! She's excited to do things. Things like mini-golf!

"Can we go play mini-golf right now? Right now!" Maria says.

"Sure, we can do that first." José says.

José, Maria, and Oscar walk to the mini-golf part of the park. They buy a game of mini-golf. They then get their balls and clubs. From here, they can start! They go to the first hole.

"I'm going to beat you!" Maria says to both brothers.

"I don't think so!" José says.
The game continues. One hole after another, they slowly make their way to the end of the course. Maria is happy because this is a game where she can keep up with her brothers. With most sports it would be hard, because she is so much smaller. With mini-golf, it is more level.

It's so level, in fact, that when they finish the ninth hole, Maria wins after all! She starts gloating to her two brothers. "Did you see that? I won!" Maria says.

"Nobody likes a sore winner!" Oscar says.

"Okay, kids, calm down!" José says. "Shall we go to the go-karts now?"

"Yeah, I want to beat Oscar again!" Maria says.

"Shut up!" Oscar says.

"Maria, riding go-karts is not a race. You are not beating anybody. You are just trying to have fun and go as fast as you can!" José says.

"That sounds less fun than beating Oscar." Maria says.

"You will have fun. Come on!" José says.

They all walk to the go-kart building. In front of the go-kart building is a really big track where there are already people racing. Maria gets nervous. They're going so fast!

The three children walk up to the cart vendor. "Hello, we need three carts please."

"How old is she?" the cart vendor says, pointing at Maria.

"She's 12 years old." José says.

"I'm sorry, you have to be 13 to ride in a single cart," the cart vendor says.

Maria gets sad. She may be nervous, but that doesn't mean she isn't excited.

"Well, can she ride with me?" José says.

"How old are you?" asks the cart vendor.

"I'm 16 years old." he says.

"Do you have a driver's license with you?" the cart vendor asks.

"Yes. Here you go." He grabs his wallet and takes out his license.

The woman looks at it. "Okay. I need you to sign this waiver."

"Absolutely." José says.

Maria becomes really happy again. She gets to ride in a go-kart after all. She can't wait to speed around the track and see the trees become a blur around her!

"Okay, you guys are good to go. Go to the waiting area. You two will be in double cart 14, and you will be in single cart 3." the cart vendor says. The children do as they're told. They go to the waiting area. It has never been so hard to wait! They're all impatient to get on the track and start driving.

"Wow! It's hot." Oscar says.

"It won't be in a second, brother. The wind and speed cool you down." José responds.

"That doesn't do anything right now!" Oscar says.

"Stop complaining!" Maria says. She punches her brother in the arm playfully. He laughs and so does she.

"I complain when I want to complain!" Oscar says.

"I see that!" Maria says.

Finally, the line starts moving again. The people that were just on the track are coming back and pulling in. The guy at the finish line says, "Thank you, please come back" to everybody. Maria wonders if they will.

When everybody that was in a cart is out, another man stands up. He looks like the man at the finish line. He helps people get into their carts. He looks at the stamps on the hands of the three children, then takes them to their carts.

Maria and José get into their cart. José is at the steering wheel. The man buckles them both in, and pulls Maria's extra tight. "Safety first!" he says. He then turns the key. The go-kart comes to life.

The man at the finish line picks up a sign. It says "stop". He stands to the side of the track. When all the go-karts are running, he says "On 3, you can go." Then, he counts!

1...
2...

3!

Maria and José take off. They're going very fast. Maria can't remember if she's ever gone this fast before! She certainly doesn't think so. They do a few laps and then the ride ends. The man who held the stop sign is now holding a sign that says, "Slow down, final lap". José and Maria pull into the waiting area again and wait for the man to unbuckle them.

"Did you have fun?" José says.

"So much!" Maria says.

José smiles because he knows he has done a good job as a brother. Maria smiles too because she likes to go fast.

They get out and meet with Oscar.

"How was it, Oscar?" José asks.

"Super fun! I'm glad we did it." Oscar says.

"Me, too." José says. "Mom and dad are probably worried! Let's find them."

The three go to the pond where they see their mother and father feeding ducks, just like they said.

"The ducks are funny today!" the father says.

"The ducks are always funny, they're ducks!" Oscar says.

"Is there anything you kids want to do before we leave?" the mother says.

Maria looks out at the park. "Can we walk the trail?"

The mother smiles. "Absolutely."

The mother and father stand up. Maria walks towards the trail and the rest follow. Maria slows down so the others can catch up.

They walk around the trail and look out at the beautiful pond too. They think about how perfect the day is, even if it is a little bit hot. In the sky, they hear birds sing. Maria thinks about how she wants to be a singer. Her father says "that will be you!". Maria laughs.

"I am lucky! We are all lucky." Maria says.

"Why is that?" José asks.

"Because family is everything!" Maria answers.

At this point, they finish the trail and walk to the car. Father drives them home, and everybody is smiling or taking a nap.

Grammar Notes/Vocab

The biggest thing to take away from this chapter is working with irregular verbs such as *tener* (as mentioned in the previous chapter), *hacer*, and *ir*. All of these are very important, *ir* especially, as it means *to go*. *Hacer* is also an incredibly multifaceted verb. That you will need to acquaint yourself with, and it means *to do* or *to make*. The last verb that you really need to work with in this chapter is *poder*, meaning *to be able to*. *Poder* is often conjugated in an imperfect form in order to mean something along the lines of "could" in English, as in "could we?" or "We could do *x*"; essentially a hyper-polite word that you need to learn.

Ir

yo	voy
tú	vas
él/ella/usted	va
nosotros	vamos
ellos/ellas/ustedes	van

Hacer

yo	hago
tú	haces
él/ella/usted	hace
nosotros	hacemos
ellos/ellas/ustedes	hacen

Poder

yo	*puedo*
tú	*puedes*
él/ella/usted	*puede*
nosotros	*podemos*
ellos/ellas/ustedes	*pueden*

Vocab:

soleado	-	sunny
absolutamente	-	absolutely
azul	-	blue
calor	-	hot
segundo	-	second
hermano	-	brother
ciudad	-	city
cielo	-	sky/heaven
brillante	-	brilliant

Chapter 4: *Salvador Poutine Day*

In Spanish

En la cultura latinoamericana, la familia es una gran cosa. De hecho, hay un dicho: *la familia lo es todo*. Las familias son muy apretadas en América Latina, y se aman mucho.

El Día de la Madre se acercaba, y María y sus hermanos querían dar un descanso a su madre.

"¡Lo sé!" dijo María. "¿Por qué no le preparamos una comida?"

"¡Sí!" dijo Óscar. "Podemos decirle que se relaje. Entonces, cocinaremos una gran comida para ella."

"Me gusta esa idea." dijo José. "Mamá nunca tiene un descanso. Realmente se lo merece."

Así que le contaron a su madre el plan que habían inventado.

"¿Estás seguro de que puedes manejar cocinar una comida tan grande como esa?" preguntó su madre.

"Por supuesto, mamá. José es casi un adulto. Él puede asegurarse de que no hagamos nada mal" dijo María.

"Bueno, esta bien. ¡Sería bueno tomar un descanso!" dijo su madre.

"**No te preocupes** por nada, mamá. ¡El Día de la Madre va a ser tu día!" dijo María.

Al día siguiente, María y sus hermanos trataron de decidir qué querían cocinar.

"¡Hay tantas cosas que podríamos hacer!," dijo María.

"Bueno, vamos a dar un paso a la vez," dijo José.

"Bien bien. Pero ¿podemos hacer una comida tradicional salvadoreña, como mamá hubiera tenido en casa?", preguntó María.

"Si seguro. Te enseñaré a dos cómo hacer tamales. Nuestra abuela me enseñó cuando era muy joven," dijo José.

"¿No todos los países latinoamericanos tienen tamales?" **preguntó** Oscar.

"Sí, pero El Salvador es específicamente conocido por sus tamales," dijo José.

Y así todos ellos decidieron que harían muchos tamales para su plato principal.

-¿Qué vamos a tener al lado? -preguntó Oscar.

"Bueno, hay muchos platos tradicionales que podríamos hacer. Pero creo que deberíamos mantenerlo sencillo y hacer **arroz** y **frijoles** ," dijo José.

"Oh, ¿podemos hacer horchatas también? Mamá ama horchatas," dijo María.

"Está bien, podemos hacer horchatas," dijo José.

Así que allí tenían su plan de juego. Iban a hacer un montón de tamales para toda la familia y servirlos con grandes ollas de arroz y frijoles! Justo al lado de todo lo demás sería una gran jarra llena de delicioso horchata. Todos los niños estaban entusiasmados con su plan.

Queriendo sorprender a su madre con sus planes de cena, fueron a ver a su padre para pedirle que les comprara los ingredientes.

"Padre, ¿nos comprarías los ingredientes para tamales y horchata, además de arroz y frijoles?" preguntó María.

"Por supuesto, ¡pero tendrás que decirme exactamente lo que necesitas!" dijo papá.

"¡Podemos hacer eso!" dijo Oscar.

"Bueno. ¿Qué **necesitas**?" preguntó papá.

"Ah ... Hm." Oscar estaba **confundido**, y le pidió ayuda a su hermano José.

"No estoy seguro de lo que necesitamos -dijo José-.

"Necesitamos buscar algunas recetas," dijo María. -Entonces podemos decirle exactamente lo que necesitamos, papá -dijo María-.

"Eres una chica inteligente, María" dijo papá. "Si todos regresan con una lista de los ingredientes que necesitan, entonces absolutamente iré a buscarlos para ustedes."

Esto hizo felices a los niños. Fueron a la habitación de José, y él puso en marcha su computadora para que pudieran buscar en internet recetas.

Después de buscar un poco, descubrieron que necesitarían muchas cosas diferentes. **Por ejemplo**, para la horchata, necesitarían arroz, **canela**, **leche**,

vainilla y **azúcar**. Mientras tanto, para los tamales salvadoreños, necesitarían **pollo**, **tomates**, **patatas**, **cebolla**, **zanahoria**, **apio**, cilantro, **hojas de plátano** y **harina de masa**. Además de esto, por supuesto, que necesitan su arroz y frijoles para el lado.

Cuando supieron lo que necesitaban, hicieron una última para su padre. Entonces le llevaron la lista.

"¿Cómo te parece esto, papá?"-preguntó María.

"Voy a ir a buscarlo todo mañana después del trabajo," dijo Papá.

Los niños estaban contentos! Ellos iban a llegar a hacer que su madre la cena del Día de la Madre que querían y ella sería muy feliz por ello. Pasó el resto del día y los niños se acostaron. No podían esperar a que pasaran los próximos días y llegara finalmente el Día de la Madre.

El día antes del Día de la Madre, María se dio cuenta de algo importante. Ella consiguió a sus hermanos y les dijo: "Tenemos que empezar en la horchata!"

Todos fueron a la cocina. Tienen un procesador de comida y poner el arroz y un par de palos de canela en ella. Luego agregaron un par de tazas de agua. Luego se mezclaron hasta que el arroz era grueso en el agua. Luego añadieron un poco más de agua al arroz-agua y lo pusieron en la nevera para que los sabores pudieran combinarse.

Todos ellos no pensaron nada más y siguieron sus días. ¡El día siguiente era cuando la diversión comenzaría! Cuando María se iba a la cama, apenas podía esperar. De hecho, ella no pensaba que iba a dormir un guiño! Ella estaba emocionada de hacer su cena mamá, por supuesto. Sin embargo, estaba más emocionada porque nunca había hecho la cena sin la ayuda de sus padres o abuelos. Para ella, era un gran paso, y probaría que estaba creciendo.

Finalmente, María se durmió, al igual que la luna, y el sol volvió a levantarse al día siguiente. María se levantó de la cama y fue a buscar a sus hermanos. Todos bajaron y felicitaron a su madre y le agradecieron por todo lo que había hecho.

La familia se sentó y se divirtió un rato. Luego, cuando llegó la cena, los niños fueron a la cocina y se pusieron a trabajar. En primer lugar, tenían que hacer un caldo de verduras que podían cocinar su pollo pulg. Ponían todas las verduras en una olla grande y luego hervía un poco para que los sabores pudieran mezclarse.

Mientras los sabores se mezclaban, decidieron terminar la horchata. Sacaron la mezcla de arroz y agua de la nevera y luego sacaron el arroz, vertiendo el agua de arroz en un recipiente grande. A este recipiente, agregaron mucha leche, azúcar y vainilla. Se revolvieron y luego lo probaron. Mmmm! Estaba delicioso. Lo pusieron en la nevera para que pudiera enfriarse.

Cuando la horchata se terminó y el caldo se hizo a fuego lento, ponen el pollo en ella y luego poner la tapa de nuevo. Ellos cocinaron el pollo durante mucho tiempo hasta que estaba muy tierna. Mientras el pollo estaba cocinando, decidieron hacer sus cáscaras de maíz.

Sacaron todo lo que necesitaban: su harina de maca, su manteca de cerdo y su caldo. Sin embargo, la bolsa de harina de maca era demasiado pesada para María, y todo se derramó.

“¡Oh, no, María! Eso fue toda la harina de maca que teníamos!" dijo Oscar.

"Voy a empezar a limpiar," dijo José.

María se disculpó mucho.

"¿Qué vamos a hacer ahora? ¡No podemos hacer tamales!" dijo María.

"Bueno, tal vez podamos hacer otra cosa," dijo Oscar.

“¿Cómo qué?” dijo María.

"Tenemos cocina de pollo. ¿Por qué no usamos el pollo y las verduras en otra cosa?" dijo Oscar.

"Hm, ¿por qué no hacemos nuestra propia receta?" Preguntó María.

Y así lo hicieron. Buscaron en la cocina para cualquier otra cosa que pudieran agregar para hacer una gran comida. Cortaron y frieron las patatas restantes en una sartén, luego cubrieron las papas fritas con el pollo y las verduras. Después, pusieron algo de queso fresco fresco (queso fresco).

“¡Es como poutine!” dijo Óscar, finalmente terminando de limpiar el desorden.

“Entonces lo llamaremos Salvador Poutine” dijo María.

Cuando todo estaba listo, había un gran plato de Salvador Poutine en medio de la mesa. María, Oscar y José estaban nerviosos para ver si su madre quería la comida, ya que no resultó como querían.

Llamaron a su madre y su padre. Su padre miró la mesa.

"¡Pensé que ustedes estaban haciendo tamales!" Dijo su padre.

"Decidimos hacer a Salvador Poutine en su lugar," dijo Oscar.

"Salvador Poutine, ¿eh?" Dijo su padre.

"¡Sí, lo creamos!" Dijo María.

"¿Lo hiciste?" preguntó su madre.

"¡Sí!" Dijo María.

Todos se sentaron alrededor de la mesa. El padre de los niños dijo gracia, añadiendo algo extra sobre lo agradecidos que estaban todos por la madre.

"¡Entramos!" dijo su padre.

Los niños observaron a su madre para ver cómo le gustaría la comida que hicieron para ella. Estaban nerviosos para ver si le gustaría. Ella tomó su primer bocado, y entonces -

"¡Yum, es delicioso! " dijo su madre.

Los niños estaban aliviados. Le dijeron a su madre que la querían, y ella lo dijo de vuelta. Domingo en su casa es ahora el día de Salvador Poutine.

In English

In Latin American culture, family is a big deal. In fact, there is a saying: *family is everything*. Families are very tight in Latin America, and they love each other very much.

Mother's Day was coming up, and Maria and her brothers wanted to give their mother a break.

"I know!" said Maria. "Why don't we cook her a meal?"

"Yes!" said Oscar. "We can tell her to relax. Then, we will cook a big meal for her."

"I like that idea," said José. "Mom never gets a break. She really deserves one."

And so they told their mother the plan they came up with.

"Are you sure that you can handle cooking a big meal like that?" their mother asked.

"Of course, Mom. José is almost an adult. He can make sure we don't do anything wrong," Maria said.

"Well, okay. It would be nice to take a break!" their mother said.

"Don't worry about a thing, mama. Mother's Day is going to be your day!" Maria said.

The next day, Maria and her brothers tried to decide what they wanted to cook.

"There are so many things that we could make!" Maria said.

"Well, let's take it one step at a time." José said.

"Okay, okay. But can we make a traditional El Salvadoran food, like mama would have had back home?" Maria asked.

"Yes, sure. I'll teach you two how to make tamales. Our grandma taught me when I was very young." José said.

"Doesn't every Latin American country have tamales?" Oscar asked.

"Yes, but El Salvador is specifically known for their tamales!" José said.

And so, they all decided that they would make a lot of tamales for their main course.

"What will we have on the side?" Oscar asked.

"Well, there are a lot of traditional dishes that we could make. But I think we should keep it simple and just make rice and beans." José said.

"Oh, can we make horchatas too? Mom loves horchatas." Maria said.

"Sure, we can make horchatas." José said.

So, there they had their game plan. They were going to make a bunch of tamales for the whole family and serve them with big pots of rice and beans! Right beside everything else would be a big pitcher full of delicious horchata. All the children were excited about their plan.

Wanting to surprise their mother with their dinner plans, they went to their father to ask him to buy them the ingredients.

"Father, would you buy us the ingredients for tamales and horchata, as well as some rice and beans?" Maria asked.

"Of course, but you're going to have to tell me exactly what you need!" Papa said.

"We can do that!" Oscar said.

"Okay. What do you need?" Papa asked.

"Ah... Hm." Oscar was confused, and he asked his brother José for help.

"I'm not sure what we need." José said.

"We need to look for some recipes!" Maria said. "Then we can tell you exactly what we need, papá." Maria said.

"You're a smart girl, Maria." Papa said. "If you all come back with a list of the ingredients that you need, then I will absolutely go and get them for you."

This made the children happy. They went to José's room, and he started up his computer so that they could look on the internet for recipes.

After searching for a little bit, they found out that they would need a lot of different things. For example, for the horchata, they would need *rice, cinnamon, milk, vanilla,* and *sugar.* Meanwhile, for the Salvadoran tamales, they would need *chicken, tomatoes, potatoes, onion, carrot, celery, cilantro, plantain leaves,* and *masa flour.* On top of this, of course, they would need their *rice* and *beans* for the side.

When they knew what they needed, they made a last for their father. They then took him the list.

"How does this sound, papá?" Maria asked.

"I'll go to get everything tomorrow after work." Papá said.

The children were happy! They were going to get to make their mother the Mother's Day dinner they wanted and she would be very happy about it. The rest of the day went by and the children went to bed. They couldn't wait for the next few days to pass and for Mother's Day to finally arrive.

The day before Mother's Day, Maria realized something important. She got her brothers and told them "We have to start on the horchata!"

They all went to the kitchen. They got a food processor and put the rice and a couple cinnamon sticks in it. Then they added a couple cups of water. Then they blended until the rice was chunky in the water. Then they added a little more water to the rice-water and put it in the fridge so that the flavors could combine.

They all thought nothing more of it and went on about their days. The next day was when the fun would begin! When Maria was going to bed, she could barely wait. In fact, she didn't think she would sleep a wink! She was excited to make her mom dinner, of course. However, she was more excited because she had never made dinner without the help of her parents or grandparents. To her, it was a big step, and would prove that she was growing up.

Eventually, Maria did fall asleep, and so did the moon, and the sun rose again the following day. Maria lept out of bed and went to go get her brothers. They all went downstairs and congratulated their mother and thanked her for all that she'd done.

The family sat together and had fun for a while. Then when dinner came around, the kids went to the kitchen and got to work. First, they had to make a vegetable broth that they could cook their chicken in. They put all the vegetables in a big pot and then simmered for a bit so the flavors could mix.

While the flavors mixed, they decided that they should finish the horchata. They got the rice-water mixture out of the fridge and then strained out the rice, pouring the rice-water into a big container. To this container, they added a lot of milk, sugar, and vanilla. They stirred, and then they tasted it. Mmmm! It was delicious. They put it in the fridge so that it could chill.

When the horchata was finished and the broth was done simmering, they put the chicken in it then put the lid back on. They cooked the chicken for a long time until it was very tender. While the chicken was cooking, they decided to make their corn shells.

They got out everything they needed - their maca flour, their lard, and their broth. However, the bag of maca flour was too heavy for Maria, and everything spilled out.

"Oh, no, Maria! That was all the maca flour we had!" said Oscar.

"I'll start cleaning up." said José.

Maria apologized a lot.

"What are we going to do now? We can't make tamales!" said Maria.

"Well, maybe we can make something else." said Oscar.

"Like what?" said Maria.

"We have chicken cooking. Why don't we use the chicken and the vegetables in something else?" said Oscar.

"Hm, why don't we make our own recipe?" Maria asked.

And so they did. They searched the kitchen for whatever other things they could add to make a great meal. They cut and fried the remaining potatoes in a skillet, then covered the fried potatoes with the chicken and vegetables. Afterwards, they put in some fresh traditional cheese (*queso fresco*).

"It's a little like poutine!" Oscar said, finally finished cleaning up the mess.

"Then we'll call it *Salvador Poutine*." Maria said.

When everything was ready, there was a big plate of Salvador Poutine on the middle of the table. Maria, Oscar, and José were nervous to see if their mother would like the meal, since it didn't turn out like they wanted.

They called their mother and father in. Their father looked at the table.

"I thought you guys were making tamales!" their father said.

"We decided to make Salvador Poutine instead." Oscar said.

"Salvador Poutine, huh?" their father said.

"Yeah, we created it!" Maria said.

"Did you?" their mother asked.

"Yes!" Maria said.

They all sat around the table. The children's father said grace, adding in some extra about how thankful they all were for the mother.

"Let's dig in!" their father said.

The children watched their mother to see how she would like the food they made for her. They were nervous to see if she would like it. She took her first bite, and then -

"Yum! This is delicious!" their mother said.

The children were relieved. They told their mother they loved her, and she said it back. Every Sunday at their house is now Salvador Poutine day.

Grammar Notes/Vocab

Aside from the food names, there's not a whole lot of vocab in this lesson. Rather, the big focus of this story is that we changed how we were telling the story. Instead of the story taking place in the present tense, as the first and second prose pieces did, this one shifts it to the typical mode of storytelling, where it's in the past. This gives the story a very "once upon a time" feel. So, what exactly is this tense?

In Spanish, there are two main verb tenses uses in narration. The *preterite* and the *imperfect* are their names, each with their own individual set of uses.

The *preterite* can best be described as the tense to use when describing actions that are over and done with. They take place and then they're finished - end of story. There is no sense of continuation to them. These are actions like "I picked up the phone" or "He ran 3 miles".

The *imperfect* is more of a continuative verb tense. When the imperfect is used, what it generally means is that you're giving a sense of continuation to the action, or describing something that occurred over the *course* of this action.

The phrase "When I was 17" would use the imperfect, as it describes something which happens over a course of time. "When I was 17, I would *run every day*," or "I *was working* at the docks when..." are both examples of sentences which use the *imperfect*.

This story uses almost *entirely* the preterite. The preterite is the simplest form of past tense in Spanish, so that makes this story easy. In order to form the preterite, all that you do is drop the verb stem (the -er, -ar, or -ir at the end of the verb) and add the ending relevant to the subject.

If the verb ends with an -ar, then you'll affix the following endings:

Yo	*-é*
Tú	*-aste*
Él, ella, usted	*-ó*
Nosotros	*-amos*
Ellos, ellas, ustedes	*-aron*

And if it ends with an -er or -ir, then you'll use *these* endings instead:

Yo	*-í*
Tú	*-iste*
Él, ella, usted	*-ió*
Nosotros	*-imos*
Ellos, ellas, ustedes	*-ieron*

And it's as simple as that. You can see these endings on verbs throughout this chapter.

Here's the relevant vocab from this chapter:

No te preocupes	-	don't worry
Preguntar	-	*to ask*
Arroz	-	rice
Necesitar	-	*to need*
Confundido/a	-	confused
Por ejemplo	-	for example
Vainilla	-	vanilla
Azúcar	-	sugar
Pollo	-	chicken
Tomates	-	tomatoes
Patatas	-	potatoes
Cebolla	-	onion
Zanahoria	-	carrot
Apio	-	celery
Hojas de plátano	-	plantain leaves
Harina de masa	-	corn flour

And with that, we've officially brought the short stories in this book to a close. There are, of course, a *lot* of words in this book for you to learn. However, I picked out vocab words that specifically may be of use to you as a new language learner and that will, hopefully, help you stay on track on your second read through the book.

Conclusion

Thank for making it through to the end of *Learn Spanish: Short Stories for Beginners to Learn Spanish Fast and Easy*, let's hope it was informative and able to provide you with all the tools you need to achieve your goals whatever they may be.

The next step is to keep reading, both this book and others. What I've done in this book is going to be immensely valuable to you as a Spanish learner and a language learner in general. See, we broke it down into individual steps and concepts and talked about the biggest things as they came. This allows us to tap into your natural ability to pick up language instead of relying on some sort of crutch or some sort of memory game in order to remember the language.

Playing "guess" with essential words in a language has never been fun to me. So why would we leave it up to guesswork? When you learn language in the traditional way, where you sift through lists of vocabulary, you aren't truly *learning* the language. Rather, you're learning how to *memorize certain words* and then regurgitate them. Sure, maybe that works in a general sense, but when it comes to a practical knowledge of the language, you're going to be pretty much lost.

This is because language learning is as much of an individualized art as a rigid science. There are certain things that can cause you to learn languages faster and more efficiently. This is why certain methods are rated above others and why, for example, the Pimsleur method is constantly seen as highly preferable to buying Rosetta Stone.

However, it feels like common sense to me that the best way to pick up language is by actually making yourself *communicate*. This book is hard to get through. I'm well aware - it's intentionally made to be hard to get through the first time and, perhaps, even the second. The first time, as I said at the beginning, you should be focusing on the big ideas and getting through what you can. You can't expect yourself to know every single word in the book of a language that you don't even know. Rather, when you read through a language you don't know with only tidbits of what you *do* understand, your brain naturally acclimates to that language.

I'm sure that you remember the idea of *context clues* from middle school to help you determine the meaning of a word that you don't know. Our brains are extremely adept at using context clues in all kinds of amazing ways, not the least of which is a super grand-scale sort of context clues that it uses to figure out language.

So yes, the first read was confusing, and it's likely that the second read will be as well. However, the more that you come back, and the more you try to understand, the more that those parts of your brain that naturally process language will be picking up not only the *various words in this book*, but the patterns and tendencies of the Spanish language itself. And that, as a new language learner, is something you should be striving for.

In the end, I think that I've made a really solid book and that you, as the end user and the hopeful language learner, will benefit greatly from it. That, of course, is my intent. If I was right in that, then I'd really appreciate if you were to leave me an Amazon review. Reviews help me know there's an audience and keep me producing quality content.

I'd like, just one last time, to wish you the best of luck on your journey to learning Spanish. It will be hard but, ultimately, it will most definitely be worth it. I genuinely hope that you will find this book to be an incredibly valuable asset as you push forward.

Description

Are you looking for a fantastic and in-depth way to learn a new language? Why not treat your brain and go about it the natural way? That's right, your brain has a natural way of learning language, and you simply aren't taking advantage of it.

Our brains are hardwired to act on a complex system of concepts and context clues in order to figure out language. This is why most polyglots in the world will tell you that the absolute best way to learn a language is by simply immersing yourself in it.

With this book, you'll be going through different short stories, all of which following the story of a girl named Maria and her kind family from El Salvador. Throughout the short stories, you'll be challenged and pushed to your limits - that's how you know the method is working. You'll never be left in the dust, but you will most certainly be immersed in the beautiful Spanish language. After every short story, there's an English version, in case you got totally lost, and a section with grammar tips and vocabulary to help you round out every short story with a proper lesson.

So, what are you waiting for? Start learning language the natural way by immersing yourself in these dynamic short stories.

Free membership into the Mastermind Self Development Group!

For a limited time, you can join the Mastermind Self Development Group for free! You will receive videos and articles from top authorities in self development as well as a special group only offers on new books and training programs. There will also be a monthly member only draw that gives you a chance to win any book from your Kindle wish list!

If you sign up through this link http://www.mastermindselfdevelopment.com/specialreport you will also get a special free report on the Wheel of Life. This report will give you a visual look at your current life and then take you through a series of exercises that will help you plan what your perfect life looks like. The workbook does not end there; we then take you through a process to help you plan how to achieve that perfect life. The process is very powerful and has the potential to change your life forever. Join the group now and start to change your life!
http://www.mastermindselfdevelopment.com/specialreport

You will also love these other great titles from Mastermind Self Development!

You will want to check out these other great titles Mastermind Self Development. All available in the Kindle store or you can just click on covers below.

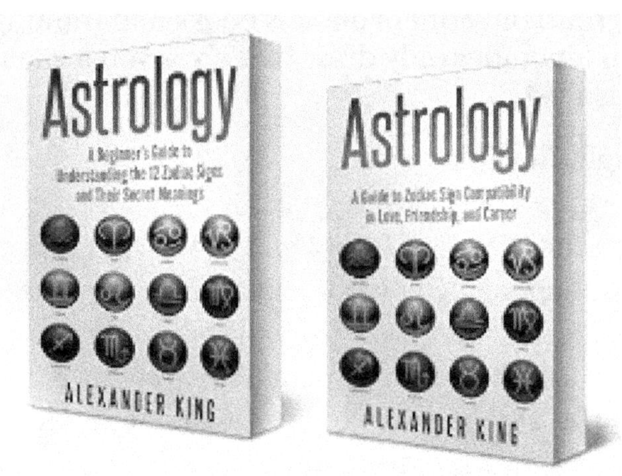

http://getbook.at/Astrology2in1

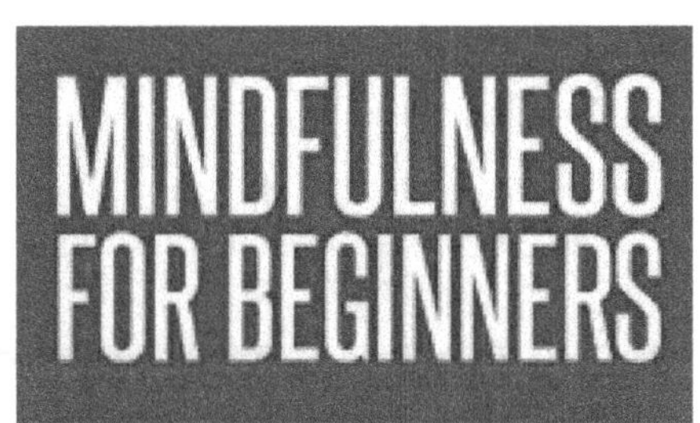

ROBERT NORMAN

http://viewbook.at/mindfulnesscombo

You can also find these titles by searching them in the Kindle store on Amazon.

Learn French:

The Best Way to Learn French

Free membership into the Mastermind Self Development Group!

For a limited time, you can join the Mastermind Self Development Group for free! You will receive videos and articles from top authorities in self development as well as a special group only offers on new books and training programs. There will also be a monthly member only draw that gives you a chance to win any book from your Kindle wish list!

If you sign up through this link http://www.mastermindselfdevelopment.com/specialreport you will also get a special free report on the Wheel of Life. This report will give you a visual look at your current life and then take you through a series of exercises that will help you plan what your perfect life looks like. The workbook does not end there; we then take you through a process to help you plan how to achieve that perfect life. The process is very powerful and has the potential to change your life forever. Join the group now and start to change your life! http://www.mastermindselfdevelopment.com/specialreport

Table of Contents

Introduction

Congratulations on downloading ***book*** and thank you for doing so.

The following chapters will discuss what is in my opinion the best and most efficient way to learn the French language.

If you're reading this, it's of course because you have an interest in learning French. There are many reasons that you may have such an interest. Maybe you've gotten a job offer which would require you to relocate to Québec or France or Morocco. Maybe you're having a hard time keeping up with your college or high school French classes and looking for some extracurricular guidance. Maybe it's just for the pure purpose of leisure and you don't really have any additional motives.

Regardless of what your goal ultimately is, my goal is to help you meet it. Throughout the course of this book, you're going to be learning quite a lot of things regarding French. In the first chapter, we'll be covering the bare essentials of sentence structure and verbiage, as well as covering essential differences between French and English. In the second, we're going to be talking more about the precise pronunciation rules of French. In the third, we're going to be talking about the past and future tenses. The fourth is going to be talking more about direct and indirect object pronouns. The fifth chapter is going to discuss higher end grammatical concepts. The fifth chapter is going to discuss basic French conversation and give you some useful phrases for travel.

There are plenty of books on this subject on the market, thanks again for choosing this one! Every effort was made to ensure it is full of as much useful information as possible, please enjoy!

Chapter 1: French - how does it work?

So many people all the time everywhere make an extreme error in learning languages: they fail to look at it in the context óf a *language* and instead try to turn it into a game of memorization. This doesn't work. There are good and bad ways to learn language, and if at the end of the day, all you have to show for yourself are a few phrases memorized off of some flash cards, then frankly, you're learning the language in a bad way.

I've been trying to communicate how to learn languages for a very long time and I'm still having a hard time determining whether I think language learning is an art or a science. Regardless, the truth is that there is no one perfect way to learn a language, because we all learn in terribly different ways, which makes it nigh impossible to pin down one singular way which would most work.

However, there are certain natural mechanisms for picking up languages that people of average intelligence and greater can utilize in order to pick up language really easily.

We don't come out of the womb learning a language. We come out as a blank slate. We have the *ability* to speak language, but it's unformed; a baby born in China will learn a form of Chinese, and a baby born in England will learn English.

Babies can't read flash cards. And while our natural propensity to learn a language demonstrably goes down as a person ages, there are numerous reasons for this which aren't normally accounted for.

A child has to learn a language in order to survive and communicate, and has an easy time learning a language due to the fact that it's completely immersed in it.

There are language learning gurus out there who are polyglots because they put themselves in similar situations in order to learn language: the immerse themselves near entirely in the language by traveling from place to place and making it so that they have to speak and understand the language to survive and communicate.

Now, it's likely not feasible for you to up and relocate to Quebec or France just in order to learn a language. But that's not to say that we can't trigger the same sort of intuitive language learning processes that these language learning gurus and these children are tapping into.

In other words, this entire method is based around the idea that if you have the proper springboard and the proper background, you can do any number of things with the language that you wish simply by natural self guided immersion and active effort in learning the language.

My goal in this book isn't to give you a vocabulary list to memorize, nor is it to give you a precise grammatical explanation of every single thing (though I'll certainly try to give accurate and succinct explanations), but rather it's to help you streamline the natural language learning processes so that you don't, well, forget every last thing that you learn in the process of reading this book.

The way that they taught you to learn languages in high school was wrong. Cut and dry, 100%, it was not the right way to go about it. Well, it was and it wasn't. It was right in some capacities - you likely had to listen to and repeat phrases in the class, which was solid basic immersion. But the idea of regurgitating vocab words onto a test is bizarre and ludicrous and just a way to ensure that you forget the very words you learned the following year.

The only way to avoid this sort of situation is by actively using the vocabulary and words that you've learned, but the reality is that a lot of high schools - especially ones with less funding - don't try particularly hard with their pen pal projects or anything of that nature.

Anyhow, the purpose of this book is to *streamline* the process of learning a language intuitively. There are a few different ways in which I'm going to try earnestly to do this. The first is by explaining the *differences* between English and French.

You may be wondering, "why would you do that? Why not start with the similarities?"

Well, the simple answer is because any language has more happening in common with another language than it has happening differently. This may sound bizarre, but think about it - every language is just a form of communication. There are various differences between them but ultimately they're all attempting to accomplish the same essential key concept: the usage of verbal cues in order to denote or tell a given thing.

However, for all the similarities, languages can also be incredibly *different*. For example, if I were going to try to tell the similarities between English and Japanese, the list would be incredibly short, by mere virtue of the fact that English and Japanese have little truly in common. Grammatically, they are incredibly different beasts. On top of this, the vocabulary is very different. It's much easier to make you understand the ways in which Japanese and English *are* different than try to expect you to latch onto the things that are.

When you're told things that are similar between languages, you latch onto those concepts. You're unaware of the vast amount of differences and you may, in fact, make very simple mistakes. One common such mistake in French is the combination of the existence and state verb *être* with the present participle of another verb.

In English, we use this to construct the present continuous tense. For example:

I *am eating.*

He *is playing.*

They *are walking.*

However, this isn't such the case in French. The equivalent phrases would be along the lines of:

Je *suis mangant.*

Il *est jouant.*

Ils *sont marchant.*

But this isn't correct at all, and in fact sound particularly bizarre and out of place to other French speakers. The correct way would be to conjugate the infinitive of the directly referenced verb (to eat, to play, to walk) for the present indicative and completely leave the *être* (to be) verb out of it:

Je *mange.*

Il *joue.*

Ils *marchent.*

There are a great number of differences between English and French as such that you'll somewhat naturally pick up as we go along, but that I'll point out regardless.

We'll be getting a lot more into the exact pronunciation of the given sounds in French in the next chapter, but for right now, I just want to give you some phrases and verbs that you can work with *as we speak.* Throughout this book, I'm going to be giving you pronunciation guides where possible. Some sounds are hard to approximate without using a phonetic alphabet, however.

One particular sound is the sound made in "je" and "le" and similar words. You may be tempted, especially if you have experience in other Romance languages where the sounds are very cut and dry, to pronounce these as "jeh" and "leh", as in "JEffrey" or "LEt's go", but you can't do that. This sound is actually much closer to the *oo* sound in *book* (U.S. English).

For phonetic purposes, this specific sound will be represented with the letters *uu.*

It's also important to bear in mind going forward that every *r* in Modern French is pronounced in a very guttural trill, quite similar to the German *r*, though not quite as intense. (though it's particularly hard for a language to be anywhere near as intense as German is, truthfully.) The only exception is generally in rural communities in Quebec or among the elderly in Southern France. Otherwise, the sound is guttural and produced from airflow at the back of the throat. It can be difficult to ascertain at first, but you can find YouTube videos concerning the French *r* to help you to understand it.

So if I were to write the following phrase:

Je prends un sandwich. *(I'll take/have a sandwich.)*

I would write the pronunciation for it as such:

juu PRAHND uh(n) sand-WEECH

The *n* in parentheses denotes that the consonant should be barely uttered and heard. This is a scale which takes practice, and plays into a major part of French pronunciation, as we'll cover in the next chapter. For now, just follow my pronunciation text, because French pronunciation is an independent fish to fry that I don't want to tackle in this chapter.

There are still more differences between French and English, and it's really important to bear these in mind as you go forward, too.

First off, they are not pronounced similarly, at all. There will be several cognates that you'll run into that look quite similar to the English phrase but are pronounced nothing the same. Take, for example, the word "horrible". In French, the *h* is silent, the *r* would be guttural, and the *ble* consonant, which would sound like "bull" in English, sounds like "bluu" in French. So we go from *HOR-ih-bull* to *or-EEH-bluu. Il y a un grand différence entre les deux!* (There's a big difference between the two!)

That's not even including *false cognates* which you need to be incredibly wary of. Take for instance the word *terrible*. It also exists in French, where in a literary sense, it means something very similar to the English "terrible". However, if you were to ask a French person how they're doing, and they said "*pas terrible*", you may think they're saying "not bad" or "not terrible", but this isn't the case. In fact, *terrible* (tuu-REEH-bluu) in the colloquial sense means "great". So "*pas terrible*" really means "not great" or "not the best".

Going beyond that, a lot of things are somewhat topsy turvy in French. Take the phrase "*yaourt aux fruits*". This means "yogurt with fruit". However, "*aux*" is a contraction of "à les", meaning "to the" or "at the". The typical French word for "with" would indeed be "*avec*", as in "*Je vais aller au MGC avec mes copains*" ("I'm going to the mall with my friends."). However, "with" doesn't have as many uses in French as it does in English, and to express the innate quality of something, or the idea of something belonging to something else in a categorical sense, you use à rather than avec.

One last super important difference that we're going to cover at this given moment is saying your occupation. In English, we say "I am *a professor*" or "I am *a butcher*". However, the French leave this article out. To them, an occupation is an intrinsic quality, which somewhat makes sense if you think about it. So instead of saying "*Je suis un professeur*" (I am a professor), the French would rather say

"Je suis professeur" (literally 'I am professor').

Basic sentence structure

Anyhow, let's get to the meat of this chapter, because there's still quite a bit left to cover: subjects and verbs. This is the basis of every single sentence we speak. I'm sure that, by now, you know what a subject is. A *subject* is the word which denotes the performer of an action.

My dog **is** <u>big</u>.

In this sentence, *my dog* is the subject, where **is** is the verb (to be). Every language has a specific order in which they put subjects, objects, and verbs (an object being the *direct recipient* of an action, such as "*I* **love** <u>cats</u>", where "cats" is the object).

Subject pronouns

In English, we use sentence pronouns quite often. In fact, we use them in nearly every sentence!

Just to prove it, I'm going to type those two sentences again and underline the subject pronouns.

In English, <u>we</u> use sentence pronouns quite often. In fact, <u>we</u> use them in nearly every sentence!

So what is a sentence pronoun? A sentence pronoun is anything which replaces giving the direct name of something in the sentence. Take for example the sentence "John plays basketball."

Normally, if we've already brought John up as the topic of conversation, we can contextually replace his name and still have it be clear that we're talking about him specifically. We would do this by saying "he plays basketball."

Then, we use *we, I,* and *you* per standard, because there's not really a first or second direct *noun*. All direct nouns are by their nature in the third person. If your name were Janet, and you were asking me for directions, I wouldn't say "Janet needs to go to the light and turn left." The *you* would imply that I'm speaking *directly* to you, and the fact that I'm talking to you directly conversely implies that I need to use *you* in the first place, because the fact that I'm talking directly *to* someone and not directly *of* someone puts the sentence in the second person. Thus, I would say "You need to go to the light and turn left."

In English, we have several different subject pronouns. However, we still have less than French, miraculously.

Here are the ones that we mainly use in English:

I   -   first person singular.

you	-	second person singular.
He, she, it	-	third person singular
we	-	first person plural
they	-	third person plural

French, likewise, has numerous. They also have something we don't: a second person plural. We do have them, but they're informal and unstandardized. For example, in the Southern U.S. you may hear "y'all", and up north and in Britain you'll often hear "you guys". However, we don't have a singular word to refer to multiple people, and they do.

They also have the concept of *formality*. This means that in the second person singular formation, they will use different words depending entirely upon who they're talking to. For example, if you're talking to somebody you just met, someone older than you, or someone in a position of authority over you, you will always use the formal second-person pronoun, which coincidentally is also the second person plural. You use the informal second-person form, the equivalent of English "you" and German "du", when you're around people younger than you, family members, or people that you have met more than once.

The French pronouns are as follows:

Je (juu)	-	first person singular
Tu (too)	-	second person singular
Il/elle (il/el)	-	third person singular
Nous (noo)	-	first person plural
Vous (voo) formal	-	second person plural / first person singular
Ils/elles (il/el) *elles* for females	-	third person plural, *ils* for males/mixed gender,

If you haven't figured it out, in French, you nearly never say the last syllable. The only case in which you do is if it's followed by a vowel, and even then, there are a lot of exceptions. You'll pick up on this a lot more as you actually work with the language and discover the parameters and tendencies of it. We'll talk more about the difference between *ils* and *elles* momentarily.

On

On is a super important term in French that you're going to run into a lot. It has a direct translation to the English *one*.

When talking to a boss, one says "vous".

Quand parler au patron, on dit << vous >>.

However, it also has an implicit meaning of "we" in reference to an unspecific group.

In France, we drink wine.

En France, on boit le vin.

What's more, in colloquial French, people will often use *on* instead of *nous* in order to avoid the more verbose nous conjugations. Compare the following sentences which mean *we're going to go to the movies*:

On va aller au cinéma. (ohn va AL-ley oh seen-ey-mah, in practice the *va* and *aller* sound like one word: ohn v'AL-ley oh seen-ey-mah)

Nous allons aller au cinéma. (nooz AL-lohn AL-ley oh seen-ey-mah)

The first is much easier to say and remember. This will become far more obvious the more that you work with French and get to more complex conjugations, such as the imperfect tense.

This pronoun deserved its own place because it's very unique and doesn't quite have a direct approximate in English. It is *always* conjugated like the *il/elle* third person pronouns, as it's a third person pronoun itself.

Verb conjugation

Verbs are always conjugated in one way or another. However, English actually has one of the easiest verb conjugation systems of any language. The only thing which makes English verb conjugation particularly difficult is the tendency of it to be irregular and for there to be a lot of verbs to cover terribly specific situations. For example, take the phrase "to wait for". You would think, given the commonness of this particular verb and situation, it would be a verb of its own accord. However, this isn't the case. French, however, *does* have a verb for this - *attendre*. "J'attends mes amis." corresponds to "I'm waiting for my friends."

Anyway, English's verb conjugation is indeed rather simple. However, it still exists in some ways. The normal way that we conjugate regular verbs is to, in the raw indicative form, to add an -s to the third person singular. Like so:

I *eat*, you *eat*, he/she/it *eats*, we *eat*, they *eat*.

Or, if it's a present continuous verb, we'll use the auxiliary verb "to be" (which is irregular) before the gerund of the given verb, as we talked about earlier:

I *am eating*, you *are eating*, he/she/it *is eating*, we *are eating*, they *are eating*.

French has a more nuanced system of conjugation than English. There are more endings and forms and even tenses. The saving grace, however, is they tend to follow a pattern all on their own. Once you learn this pattern, verbs become far easier.

The present indicative and the present continuous form a singular tense in French, known simply as the *présent*, which of course means "present". The present can be conjugated in many ways but tends to follow a pattern, as you'll see momentarily.

There are three categories of French verbs: *-re* verbs, *-er* verbs, and *-ir* verbs. Most verbs are *regular*, which means that they follow specific patterns of usage and spelling. There is some contention here, in that quite a few verbs are *irregular*... including the ones which are arguably the most common.

That's not to discourage you at all, though, as even the irregular verbs follow a very similar pattern to the regular verbs. So without further ado, let's conjugate some verbs!

First, we're going to focus on *-er* verbs, with the specific example of *parler*, meaning "to speak".

Parler - *to speak*

Conjugation	Meaning	Pronunciation
Je parl*e*	I speak	Juu pahrl
Tu parl*es*	You speak	Too pahrl
Il/elle/on parl*e*	He/she/it/one speaks	Il/el/ohn pahrl
Nous parl*ons*	We speak	Noo pahr-lohn
Vous parl*ez*	You all/you (f.) speak	Voo pahr-ley
Ils/elles parl*ent*	They speak	Il/el pahrl

The way that conjugation works is by dropping the final two letters of the regular verb, always -er, -ir-, or -re, and replacing them with the given suffix. The suffixes for each pronoun are italicized.

As you can see, the endings for *-er* verbs are *-e*, *-es*, *-e*, *-ons*, *-ez*, and *-ent*.

Now is a better time than any to make a mental note for you: you do NOT pronounce the *-ent* suffix on *-er* verbs. Ever. The verb sounds functionally the same as the third person *singular* conjugation.

Anyway, now let's do an *-ir* verb. The endings for *-ir* verbs are *-is*, *-is*, *-it*, *-issons*, *-issez*, and *-issent*. You don't pronounce the *-ent* here, either. However, it doesn't sound like the third person singular, because the third person singular ends in a *t* sound (if followed by a vowel) or none at all, where the third person plural ends in an *s* sound.

Finir - *to finish*

Conjugation	Meaning	Pronunciation
Je fin*is*	I finish	Juu fee-nee
Tu fin*is*	You finish	Too fee-nee
Il/elle/on fin*it*	He/she/it/one finishes	Il/el/ohn fee-nee
Nous fin*issons*	We finish	Noo fee-nee-sohn
Vous fin*issez*	You all/you (f.) finish	Voo fee-nee-sey
Ils/elles fin*issent*	They finish	Il/el fee-nees

And lastly, we're going to work with regular -re verbs. -Re verbs can be somewhat tricky, because they change the scheme up a bit. The third person singular doesn't add *anything* to the stem. Thus, the -re verb endings are as follows: -s, -s, nothing, -ons, -ez, -ent. Let's practice this using the verb *vendre*, meaning "to sell".

Vendre - *to sell*

Conjugation	Meaning	Pronunciation
Je vend*s*	I sell	Juu vahnd
Tu vend*s*	You sell	Too vahnd
Il/elle/on vend	He/she/it/one sells	Il/el/ohn vahn
Nous vend*ons*	We sell	Noo vahnd-ohns
Vous vend*ez*	You all/you (f.) sell	Voo vahnd-ey
Ils/elles vend*ent*	They sell	Il/el vahnd

Do you see how this is working? These verbs all follow a very certain manner of spelling, but it certainly does have an order that you can really easily pick up on. And if it seems difficult now, don't worry - it will most definitely make more sense with practice.

I'd like to move onto articles, but we can't quite yet. This is because we need to cover some major *irregular* verbs. These are verbs that you may use which don't follow the same rules as the verbs prior. These are verbs that you'll learn with practice. The first one that we're going to cover is "to be", or *être*. Here's how you conjugate it.

Être - *to be*

Conjugation	Meaning	Pronunciation
Je suis	I am	Juu swee
Tu es	You are	Too ey
Il/elle/on est	He/she/it/one is	Il/el/ohn ey
Nous sommes	We are	Noo sohm
Vous êtes	You all/you (f.) are	Vooz eht
Ils/elles sont	They are	Il/el sohn

You use être pretty much as you would expect to use it. There are certain places where the translation of "to be" don't quite work across English to French, though, but we'll get there in a second.

You use être in order to describe something or somebody, as well as to tell where you are. It actually corresponds largely to "to be" in English, but there are certain cases where it does. For example, in English, we'd say "I'm 20 years old". *Mais en français*, we'd say "I have 20 years". There are a few other examples I'll list off momentarily, after going into the conjugation of "to have".

Avoir - *to have*

Conjugation	Meaning	Pronunciation
J'ai (*Je ai* contraction)	I have	Jey
Tu as	You have	Too ah
Il/elle/on a	He/she/it/one has	Il/el/ohn ah
Nous av*ons*	We have	Noo ah-vohn
Vous av*ez*	You all/you (f.) have	Voo ah-vey
Ils/elles ont	They have	Il/el ohn

So to say *I'm twenty years old* in French, you'd say *j'ai vingt ans* (jey VAHNT ahn) - "I have twenty years".

There are some embarrassing mix-ups between être and avoir which might happen. You need to be mindful and aware of these. Consider, for example, the sentence "I am full". You might be tempted to translate this directly: *je suis plein*. But this is a HORRIBLE idea! Why? Because *"Je suis plein" does* mean "I'm full"... as in "I'm full with a baby."

Instead, you'd say **J'ai** *plein*, or roughly "I have fullness".

This likewise plays out with "I'm hot". If you were to say "Je suis chaude" as a woman, you'd be telling somebody you're *aroused*. Rather, you'd want to say "J'ai chaude" - "I have hot". This means that the temperature is hot, or that you feel an uncomfortable heat.

Avoir is used for a few other phrases similarly to describe personal feelings. *J'ai faim* would mean "I'm hungry", though it literally means *I have hunger*.

The next verb we have to cover is *faire*. *Faire* technically means "to do" or "to make", but it has a ton of idiomatic expressions as well. Here's how you conjugate faire:

Faire - *to do, to make*

Conjugation	Meaning	Pronunciation
Je fais	I do, I make	Juu feh
Tu fais	You do, you make	Too feh
Il/elle/on fait	He/she/it/one does, he/she/it/one makes	Il/el/ohn feh
Nous fais*ons*	We do, we make	Noo feh-zohn
Vous faites	You all/you (f.) do, you all/you (f.) make	Voo feht
Ils/elles font	They do, they make	Il/el fohn

There are many cases where you'll use "faire", like so.

Où est Timothie? (Where is Timothy?)

Dans sa chambre. Il **fait** *ses devoirs*. (He's in his room. He's *doing* **his homework**.)

It's also has quite a few idiomatic uses. For example, if it's a nice day out, you would say "*Il fait beau*" - literally "It's doing handsome". If it's hot, you'd say "*il fait chaud*" and if it's cold, you'd say "*il fait froid*". In other words, if you're using an adjective to describe the weather, you'd use *il fait...* before it. However, if you're describing a current weather action, like rain or snow, you use the verb for those: *neiger* and *pleuvoir* specifically. "It's snowing" would be "Il neige" (Il nehj) and "It's raining" would be "Il pleut" (Il ploo).

Another verb that we need to cover is *aller*, which means "to go". You need to understand this verb in order to understand the near future tense later.

Aller - *to go*

Conjugation	Meaning	Pronunciation
Je vais	I go	Juu vey
Tu vas	You go	Too vah
Il/elle/on va	He/she/it/one goes	Il/el/ohn vah
Nous all*ons*	We go	Nooz al-LOHN
Vous allez	You all/you (p.) go	Vooz al-LEY
Ils/elles vont	They go	Il/el vohn

You would use *aller* exactly as you'd expect to. If you're going to a place, you of course would use a preposition to denote it. The preposition is generally à:

Je vais à la bibliothèque. (juu vey-z-ah lah beeb-leeh-oh-tek)

I'm going to the library.

We'll talk more about à in the chapter regarding prepositions, though.

There's one more irregular verb I'm going to specifically hop into in this chapter before we head into the next one about the wonderfully confusing world of French pronunciation: *venir*, or "to come". The cool thing about *venir* is that once you understand it, you understand the verbs which spring from it - *revenir*, meaning "to come back/come again"; *devenir*, meaning "to become"; *souvenir*, meaning "to remember". Here's how you would conjugate *venir* and its derivatives:

Venir - *to come*

Conjugation	Meaning	Pronunciation

Je viens	I come	Juu vee-ahn
Tu viens	You come	Too vee-ahn
Il/elle/on vient	He/she/it/one comes	Il/el/ohn vee-ahn
Nous venons	We come	Noo vuu-nohn
Vous venez	You all/you (p.) come	Voo vuu-ney
Ils/elles viennent	They come	Il/el vee-ehn

Venir is often paired with "de", meaning "from" or "of". Observe:

D'où viens-tu? ("Where are you from?", literally "from where are you coming?")

Je viens des États-Unis. ("I come from the United States.")

There are a few more big verbs, but we'll cover them later on in the book. For now, just try to get some practice with -er, -ir, and -re verbs. I've included some regular -er, -ir, and -re verbs in order to help you get the hang of it through practice and dedication.

insert verbs

Articles

Before we move on to the next chapter, it's absolutely necessary that we cover articles. Articles make up a huge part of French. Every single noun must have an article before it, no exceptions. Well, some exceptions, but they're very few.

What are articles? They're not what you read in the paper or on Facebook, shared by a zealous family member. No, *articles* are the part of speech which refers to the marker for a noun. That is to say, look at the following sentences:

*I eat **some** apples.*

*I eat **the** apples.*

*I eat **an** apple.*

Some, the, and *an* are the markers here, because they tell you the specificity of the thing. *Some* means that you're eating any given apples. *The* implies that you're eating a very specific, previously referenced set of apples. *An* implies that you eat any given apple.

In French, this is expanded upon, much like verb conjugation.

Before we talk about that, we need to talk about *gendered nouns*. Every noun in French has a gender. This doesn't mean that an *apple* is a woman, of course. It's not going to bear your child or anything. The genders of nouns are a totally grammatical separation - a holdover from Vulgar Latin, more or less. The genders are also intrinsic to French. A lot of words would be a lot weirder and a lot of phraseologies would be a lot stranger if gendered nouns were slowly phased out.

The idea of gendered nouns may seem extremely bizarre to an English speaker, and indeed, it can be a little strange at first. None of our nouns have genders. But after practice and dedication, you'll start to learn what makes a noun a certain gender and be able to more or less guess what gender a noun is with some degree of accuracy.

It's important to note that the gender of a noun will correlate to it in subject pronouns, like so:

"Comment tu l'aimes, la pomme?" (How do you like the apple?)

"Elle est un peu acide." (It's a tad tart.)

"Apple" is feminine - *la pomme* - and so when we reference it in the sentence following, we have to use the feminine pronoun.

Anyhow, back to the main topic of articles.

Firstly, we have *definite articles*. These correspond to "the". There are four different definite articles:

Le - masculine singular: *Le pont* ("the bridge")

La - feminine singular: *La vache* ("the cow")

Les - plural: *Les enfants* ("the children")

L' - followed by vowel: *L'art* ("the art")

You use definite articles when you're talking about a specific instance of something. Basically, in the same way that you'd use "the" in English. You also use it when you're referring to something in a broader sense, where in English we'd normally *drop* the article altogether.

For example, if you wanted to say "I like oranges", you'd use the definite articles - *J'aime les oranges* - where in English we don't use an article at all in that sentence.

After definite articles, we have *partitive* articles. These basically mean "some of" or "any". These are as follows:

Du - masculine singular: *Du vin* ("some wine")

De la - feminine singular: *De la pizza* ("some pizza")

Des - plural: *Des framboises* ("some raspberries")

De l' - before vowel: *De l'eau* ("some water")

Generally, partitive articles are used in reference to food or drink.

The last form of article in French is the *indefinite* article. This correlates to "a" or "an" in English. This has two forms:

Un - masculine singular: *Un léon* ("A lion")

Une - feminine singular: *Une langue* ("A language")

That about sums up articles in French. We can go a bit further with them, but that involves the next part, which is…

Negation

Okay, I lied. There's actually one more major thing we have to cover before we go onto the next part. That's the concept of "negation". Negation means simply taking something and then turning it negative. We negative things in English by adding "do not". For example:

"I don't like to walk."

"He doesn't talk."

"We don't look."

You can also negate things in French. You do so by surrounding the verb with *ne pas*. The *ne* indicates a negative statement, where the *pas* means specifically "not".

So to take those sentences we just wrote and translate them:

"Je **n'**aime **pas** marcher." (Juu nehm pah mahr-chey)

"Il **ne** parle **pas**." (Il nuu pahrl pah)

"Nous/on **ne** regardons/regarde **pas**." (Noo/ohn nuu ruu-gahr-dohn/ruu-gahrd pah)

See how that works?

Now, how do articles come into play? Well, if you have a negative statement, it's important to take note that the article will change if you're negating a sentence with partitive or indefinite articles. However, it doesn't change in sentences with definite articles.

Here's a sentence with an indefinite article:

J'ai une plume. (I have a pen.)

And here it is, negated:

Je n'ai pas de plume. (I don't have a pen.)

This change, however, does *not* occur in sentences with definite articles.

*As-tu vu **le** film? (Have you seen the film?)*

*Non, je n'ai vu **le** film. (No, I haven't seen the film.)*

While we're on the topic of negation, there are a few special cases where you *don't* use "ne…pas", and where "pas" actually changes.

These are as follows:

Ne…rien   -   "nothing"

Ne…jamais   -   "never"

Ne…pas encore -   "not yet"

Ne…plus   -   "not any longer"

Ne…personne -   "nobody"

So you could use these as follows:

Je ne veux rien. ("I want nothing," or "I don't want anything.")

Il ne le fait pas encore. ("He hasn't done it yet.")

Nous ne sommes contents plus. ("We aren't happy anymore.")

They're a little obtuse to learn and understand at first, but they're not too terribly difficult to grasp once you get the hang of them, and they can make your writing far more expressive, too.

Chapter 2: Pronunciation

French is a beast when it comes to pronunciation. I'm not even going to lie to you, not for a second. The hardest thing when it came to learning French for me, starting out, was listening and speaking. Reading and writing French can be a breeze once you grasp the finer points, but actually making sense of the bizarre syllabary, that's another story entirely. It can be really difficult coming from a language like English to understand all of the nuances of French pronunciation. But luckily, I'm here to try to help you through the major parts.

Liaison

The first topic we're going to cover is *liaison*. This is the idea of connecting sounds. It's part of what makes French such a beautiful and graceful language to listen to.

Somewhere along the line during the development of French, the final pronunciation of letters in words dropped for the most part. However, there are certain locations where these letters can still be heard.

Take, for example, the article *les*. By itself, it's boring - it sounds like "lay", and you don't pronounce the *s*. However, if we put a word with a vowel in front of it, like *éléphants* ("elephants", of course), the *s* in *les* is heard:

J'aime bien les éléphants. (Jehm bee-ahn lay-z-ey-ley-fahn-t)
I really like/quite like the elephants.

This is a super important concept to nail. It can be rather difficult to ascertain and follow through with at first. I remember that when I started out in French, this concept absolutely *floored* me. I had no idea what to do with this or how to apply it. After all, French spellings can often be so weird anyway - how was I supposed to remember when one is supposed to insert a consonant you wouldn't normally hear?

Well, it's a natural fear, and as with most fears, it turned out to be rather unfounded. With time and practice, I found myself to naturally pick up liaison.

There are some very specific cases for liaison, however - and some places you never use it.

Generally, you use liaison if the word preceding the vowel ends in either an *l, t, d, p, s, f, and x.* They generally sound as you'd expect, except for *f* which sounds like a *v*, *d* which sounds like a *t,* and *x* which sounds like an *s.*

There are three kinds of liaison in French: *required, forbidden,* and *optional.*

Required liaison exist in many different cases. You *have* to use liaison with these words, there is not an option as to whether you do or not. These words are generally words which are linked in some way or another. You'll use this type of liaison after pronouns (*nous allons*), between a number and a noun (*trois amis*), after prepositions which have only one preposition (*en avance*), after articles (*un orange*), after *est*, after *comment* when asking someone how they're doing (*comment allez-vous?*), between a preceding adjective and its respective noun (*bon homme*), and after monosyllabic adverbs (*très horrible*).

Then, there are *forbidden* liaison. No matter what, you don't use the liaison in these cases. You will never, ever use liaison *before* or *after* somebody's name, after et, before the word *onze* (*J'avais onze ans*), before the word "oui" (*Je lui dis "oui"*), after any sort of plural nouns, before the preposition à, after any sort of singular noun, or before an H wherein you actually *say* the h. (These don't come up often in French, though - the H is *usually* silent.)

Then, there are optional liaisons. These are liaisons which you may or may not say. There is no rule regarding these. These pop up because language is always shifting around and modifying itself throughout time. If you encounter a liaison which is out of the realm of the formerly discussed ones, it's safe to say it's an optional liaison.

French vowels

The next major thing to talk about is the French vowels. These are relatively finite compared to English vowels, but can trip you up if you don't know them. There are also more *exact* vowel sounds because the French alphabet has accents, where the English alphabet does not.

Let's start from the beginning, shall we?

a - pronounced as an "ah"
à - pronounced as an "ah"
â - pronounced as a long "ah"
e - middle of a syllable, like "eh"; end of a syllable, like "uu"
é - pronounced like "ay"
ê - pronounced like "eh"
i - pronounced like "ee"
o - pronounced like "oh"
ô - pronounced like "oh" - denotes where a letter has been dropped in the past.
u - there's no comparable English sound; say "eeh" but then round your lips as though you're saying "ooh". The resulting sound is the French *u*.
y - pronounced like "ee"

Then, there are some really important diphthongs you need to remember.

(A diphthong is a combination of two vowels in order to form a new sound.)

ai - pronounced like "eh"
au - pronounced like "oh"
eau - pronounced like "oh"
ei - pronounced like "eh"
eu - pronounced like "uu"
oeu - pronounced like "uu"
oi - pronounced like "wah"
ou - pronounced like "ooh"

French vowels are easy and relatively simple to understand, so long as you practice. Now onto the consonants.

French consonants

The consonants, you most likely know. Here are the ones which aren't so consistent with English and may trip you up.

c - before an e or an i, it will sound like an s; in any other place, it will sound like the "c" in "cool"
ç - will sound like an s always
ch - will sound like the 'sh' in 'shoe'
g - before an e or an i, it will sound like the *s* in the word "pleasure"; in any other place, it sounds like the English g.
h - normally silent
j - sounds like the French g
qu - sounds like the "c" in "cool"
s - sounds normal if at the beginning, but like a z if in the middle of two vowels.

Using these tips, you should be able to irk out French words with little difficulty.

Chapter 3: Past and Future Tenses

French is a rather easy language to learn, but the hardest thing about it when you're coming from an English speaking background is most certainly its numerous convoluted verb tenses.

There are *at least four* basic French past tenses, and just as many basic French future tenses. You can get away with, at the basic level, knowing just two of the French past tenses, and just two of the French future tenses.

Let's take these one at a time.

Passé composé

Passé composé literally means *compound past*, and is the most common past tense used in French. It's used to reference an action which has been completed at the time of speaking, or at some point in the past. It's a relatively simple tense to form.

The passé composé is made up of two parts: the *auxiliary verb*, and the *past participle*. The auxiliary verb is *normally* avoir, but it can also be être (more on that momentarily). The *past participle* is the past tense form of the word. For example, if "I'm eating" is the present continuous, then "I have eaten" is the past perfect, wherein *have* is the auxiliary verb and *eaten* is the past participle. French works similarly.

So how do you form the past participle? It's simple.

For **-ir** verbs, you drop the **-ir** and replace it with an **-i**. *Finir*, for example, would be *fini*.

For **-er** verbs, you drop the **-er** and replace it with an **-é**. Thus, *manger* would become *mangé*.

For **-re** verbs, you drop the **-re** and replace it with an **-u**. Thus, *vendre* would become *vendu*.

To form the passé composé, all you do is conjugate the auxiliary verb to the person speaking (normally *avoir*), and then get the past participle. So "I have eaten" in French would become "J'ai mangé". "He has sold the strawberries" would be "Il a vendu les fraises".

Simple enough, right? Now the question becomes "when do we use être as opposed to avoir?"

Well, there's actually a system for this: just remember DR. and MRS. VANDERTRAMP. Seriously. That's the mnemonic.

When you're using *intransitive* verbs which indicate either motion (going somewhere) or a change of state (changing in some essential way), you use *être* as your auxiliary verb.

The following are the verbs which will use être:

Devenir - to become something
Rentrer - to enter something again
Monter - to go up something (e.g., stairs)
Rester - to stay
Sortir - to leave, exit, or go out
Venir - to come
Aller - to go somewhere
Naître - to be born to somebody
Descendre - to go down something or descend
Entrer - to enter into something
Retourner - to return to something
Tomber - to fall down or trip
Revenir - to return to something or to come back
Arriver - to arrive to/at something
Mourir - to die
Partir - to leave somewhere

An important thing to note about using être as an auxiliary verb is that you must adjust the passé composé to match the gender and person. So "he left" would be "il est venu", but "she left" would be "elle est venue", and "they left" would be "ils sont venus".

This, however, is not the case when you're using *avoir* as the auxiliary verb. When using *avoir*, the subject and the participle need not agree. The past participle of avoir must, however, agree with the direct object pronoun if it's present before the verb. (More on that momentarily.)

Imparfait

So we talked about the most common French past tense. But there's another incredibly important one that we have yet to cover at all. This tense is known as the *imparfait*. The *imparfait*, or "imperfect", doesn't refer at all to a completed event. Rather, it refers to a given ongoing event or state in the past ("I was happy", "I was young") or a repeated event ("I used to watch..."). This concept doesn't have a direct correlative in English, but the English tense "past continuous" or "past progressive" can certainly get across the same exact point.

The imperfect is simple to form.

For **-er** and **-re** verbs, you just drop the ending and add *-ais, -ais, -ait, -ions, -iez,* or *-aient*.

For **-ir** verbs, you do the same, but you add an "iss" before it.

So for example, if you wanted to say "When I was young, I would play often.", you would say *"Quand j'**étais** jeune, je **jouais** souvent."*

The imperfect is notoriously difficult to master, but it will come in handy quite often for you, so it's worth teaching anyway.

These are the main cases in which you'd want to use the imperfect over the passé composé:

- Actions or states which occurred often and not just once
- Descriptions of either emotional or physical states: personal feelings, one's age, the given time and weather.
- Any states or actions where the duration is ongoing but unknown.
- Used alongside the passé composé in order to give more depth or information.
- Polite suggestion and wishes - "Pourrais-tu m'aider?" : "Could you help me?" (literally "Would you have the ability to give me help?")
- As part of a conditional clause.

Futur Proche

Futur proche literally means "close future" and refers to events which will most certainly happen, and soon. The futur proche is insanely easy to create. All that you do is combine *aller* (to go) conjugated to the person alongside the infinitive of the verb to be carried out in the near future.

Je vais faire les magasins.
"I'm going to go shopping."

Ils vont jouer au basket.
"They're going to go play basketball."

You can combine this, of course, with dates or times to explicitly state when an action is going to be undertaken.

Vas-tu aller à la librairie demain?
"Are you going to the bookstore tomorrow?"

This is, of course, a very simple tense, but you'll find it incredibly useful. When you're out and about and scratching surface-type conversations with native French speakers, it's unlikely that as a tourist or newcomer, you're going to need to tell them your grand far-future life goals. However, if you need to, that's what the next tense is for.

__Futur Simple__

The *simple future* tense is, well, simple. It's a very no-nonsense tense that is a little more complicated than the previous tense, and it can be quite easy to sound like you have no idea what you're talking about. However, it's worth learning anyway, because it's a rather common tense.

The futur simple just implies something that will happen at some point in the future. The way that you form it is by taking the *entire infinitive* of a verb as the stem, and then adding *-ai, -as, -a, -ons, -ez,* or *-ont* depending upon who is talking. If the verb ends in **-re**, then and only then do you remove something from the verb, taking off the final -e before adding your ending.

Note that some verbs are irregular, such as être and avoir. These have the future stems of *ser-* and *aur-*, respectively.

So let's try this with the verb *chanter*, meaning "to sing". Here's how we'd do it:

Chanter - *to sing, futur simple*

Conjugation	Meaning	Pronunciation
Je chanter*ai*	I will sing	Juu shahn-teh-reh
Tu chanter*as*	You will sing	Too shahn-teh-rah
Il/elle/on chanter*a*	He/she/it/one will sing	Il/el/ohn shahn-teh-rah
Nous chanter*ons*	We will sing	Noo shahn-teh-rohn
Vous chanter*ez*	You all/you (p.) will sing	Voo shahn-teh-rey
Ils/elles chanter*ont*	They will sing	Il/el shahn-teh-rohn

Simple enough, right? The futur simple isn't a terribly difficult tense to use in and of itself, and it's rather easy to set up.

You are halfway done!

Congratulations on making it to the halfway point of the journey. Many try and give up long before even getting to this point, so you are to be congratulated on this. You have shown that you are serious about getting better every day. I am also serious about improving my life, and helping others get better along the way. To do this I need your feedback. Click on the link below and take a moment to let me know how this book has helped you. If you feel there is something missing or something you would like to see differently, I would love to know about it. I want to ensure that as you and I improve, this book continues to improve as well. Thank you for taking the time to ensure that we are all getting the most from each other.

Chapter 4: Questions and Objects

We're going to knock out two seemingly unrelated birds with one very big stone in this chapter. In French, questions and objects actually intertwine in a way. I suppose that they intertwine in any given language, really. In a lot of conversations, you'll be talking about a given subject, and in order to carry on the conversation, you'll find it necessary to ask questions about what the other person is saying. So questions like "When did you see it?" or "How did you get in there?" or "How was it?" will naturally crop up.

That is to say that any budding French conversationalist will need both of these concepts quite handily, and I'm prepared to set you up with them.

Questions

French questions are rather easy. Every question is composed of question words. Much like in English, every proper question has a word which designates *what* exactly we're asking about.

In English, these words are *what, why, how, with whom, who, which, how many*, and *where*.

In French, the words are as follows:

Quoi - What
Quand - When
Pourquoi - Why
Quel(le)(s) - Which
Combien de - How many
Comment - How
Où - Where
Qui - Who
Avec qui - With whom

These, of course, function just like they do in English - they can be parts of normal statements, or they can be used in questions.

If used in questions, there's another phrase you need to know: *est-ce que* (pronounced EST kuu). This literally translate to "is it that?". When combined with other question words, or on its own, it signals that the statement following it is a question.

Est-ce que tu l'aimes?
Do you love him?
(literally "is it [the case] that you love him?")
Où est-ce que tu chantes?
Where do you sing?

(literally "Where is it that you sing?")

This phrase already is powerful, but sometimes you don't want such a clunky phrase. Sometimes, in fact, you can say more with less. This is when inverted questions become the go-to.

And indeed, they're a little familiar to us as English speakers. Think of it this way: let's say you walked into your living room wanting to watch a certain show, but your brother or child was there watching TV, though absentmindedly since they're also playing on their DS and seem mostly preoccupied with that. You want to change the channel. What do you do?

Well, so long as you aren't a barbarian, you'll normally ask something along the lines of:
Are you watching the TV?

Which is an inverted question. What if you just wanted to say that they were watching TV? You would instead say:
You are watching the TV.

So the "you" and the "are" were inverted in order to make the sentence into a question. French questions work similarly to this mechanism.

Let's say the same scenario happened. With the little est-ce que trick we just learned, we might be tempted to say this:
Est-ce que tu regardes la télé?

But we can make this a lot shorter and snappier. We can just invert the question:
Regardes-tu la télé?

This kind of inversion will serve you very well and explain a lot of potentially confusing sentences you'll run into.

Direct object pronouns

This is a really tedious but very necessary lesson to give. We use direct object pronouns *constantly*. Think about it: have you ever been talking about something with a friend, and then you something like "Yeah, I saw them" or "Yeah, I heard it."? The answer, of course, is yes. It would be incredibly monotonous, slightly robotic, and ultimately very creepy if we *didn't* have direct object pronouns. It would feel absolutely unnatural to say the name of something every time we brought it up. Of course, it wouldn't if that were just the way we spoke, but from *our perspective* and speaking *the way we do*, it sounds odd. Besides, it saves time. Replacing a multi-syllable name or phrase with the simple "it" or "them" or "him" saves a lot of time and effort in terms of speaking and writing.

So how do direct object pronouns in French work? Well, I'm assuming that you know how they work in English already.

In French, you correlate the previously mentioned object to the correct direct object pronoun based on perspective (is it first person? second person? third person?) and plurality (singular? plural?). Then you just throw it before the noun. (Notice how I just said "throw *it* before the noun" -- direct object pronouns at work!)

The French direct object pronouns are as follows:
me - first person singular
te - second person singular
le, **la**, **l'** - third person singular
nous - first person plural
vous - second person plural
les - third person plural

So let's say that I wanted to say "I'm giving *it* to Jeffrey." How would I do so?

Well, I first recognize the "direct object". Here, it's *it*. Then I analyze to see which word fits it: *it* refers to a singular third person object, so I'll use the third person singular. Then, we have to figure out the gender of the noun. Let's say we're giving Jeffrey a papaya. This translates to *une papaye*, which is feminine. So it's a feminine third person singular direct object. Perfect. The word is *la*.

So to say "I'm giving it to Jeffrey", knowing "it" is *la*, I just have to translate the rest, and throw the *la* before the verb, like so:

Je la donne à Jeffrey.

Honestly, explaining it makes it sound so much more difficult than it really is. In practice, it's a very easy concept to grasp and there's not a whole lot of genuine difficulty involved in it.

Indirect object pronouns

This is where it gets a bit trickier. There's a huge difference between direct object pronouns and indirect object pronouns. The *direct* object is the object which is directly affected by a given verb. The *indirect* object is the object which receives the brunt of the action of the verb.

The way I like to put it is this: without the *direct object*, there is no *verb*. Full stop. If you throw a ball, you can't *detach* the ball from the concept of *throwing*. Either you're throwing a ball, or there is nothing to be thrown. The same with sending a letter. You can't just *send nothing*. You have to have something to *be* sending. You can absolutely *not* detach the concept of the letter from the notion of *sending*.

However, this is where indirect objects are different. You can detach the indirect object from the rest. The indirect object is non-essential. You can throw a ball without throwing it *to* somebody. You can send a letter without sending it *to* somebody (though it may not go anywhere.) You can do these things *without* the existence of the indirect object. But since the indirect object is *there*, it serves to give context to the verb and the direct object, by giving them an end goal and, indeed, a thing for which and to which they're performed.

The French indirect object pronouns are as follows:

me - *to me*
te - *to you*
lui - *to him/to her*
nous - *to us*
vous - *to you all/to you (f.)*
leur - to them

So let's go back to that sentence from the direct object pronoun section: "I'm giving it to Jeffrey". We ended up getting the following:

Je la donne à Jeffrey.

So how do we get the indirect object pronoun here? We first find the preposition, which will indicate to/for whom or what the action is being performed. The preposition here is à, and the prepositional phrase is "à Jeffrey." Thus, the indirect object is Jeffrey. So that's a third person singular indirect object, and it's gender neutral in the indirect object form, so we can just take *lui* and stick it behind our verb too.

Je la lui donne.

This literally means "I'm giving it to him." Not too shabby, no?

The general rule for placement of direct and indirect object pronouns, when you have both, is that they go in alphabetical order.

Adverbial pronouns

There are a couple of other pronouns you need to be aware of. They are as follows:

y - replaces "there"; also replaces "à" and a noun.
en - replaces either a partitive article and noun ("Je mange des pommes" becomes "J'en mange") or replaces *de* followed by an indefinite article and a

noun ("J'ai envie d'une plume" becomes "J'en ai envie") which makes it particularly useful for shortening phrases of verbs which traditionally are followed by de (*se souvenir de* - to be reminded of, *avoir besoin de* - to need, *avoir envie de* - to want, and so on...)

These are called *adverbial pronouns*, and will turn out to be quite useful as you go forward with French. You'll understand the usage of them more as you practice with them and read/hear more and more French.

Ce, cela, celui, and so on

One of the most important French phrases you'll ever encounter is *c'est* (sey). It's somewhat of a catchall. For example, "C'est mon chien !" means "This is/that is/it is my dog!". "Ça, c'est mon ami, [name]" can be used to introduce one friend to another. "Ça, c'est intéressant!" means "That's interesting!". The French have such a love affair with "ça, c'est" that they'll use it places where it really doesn't belong, but you'll figure that out on your own.

C'est is a contraction of the pronoun *ce* and the verb *est*. It means approximately "it is", "this is", or "that is" depending upon the context. "Ce" just means "this" or "that". You can use it before a noun, too, to indicate a specific one. For example, "ce chien" means *this dog*. If you do this, you have to pay attention to your spelling. If it's used before a masculine noun with a vowel, you have to use *cet* instead of *ce*. If it's before a feminine noun, you must use *cette*. If it's before a plural noun, you must use *ces*.

There are some other forms, too. *Ceci* and *cela* are important for you to know - they both mean approximately "this" and "that", but can be used somewhat interchangeably. Cela contracts to the popular *ça*.

Then, there's *celui* and *celle*. *Celle* is the feminine form of *celui*. They both mean "this one" or "that one" dependent upon context, and refer to one of a specific group of different people or things in a given set.

These are important pronouns for you to know just because they're so prolific in French usage.

Chapter 5: Adjectives, Adverbs, Conjunctions, and

Prepositions

Before we get to the conversational pillars of French, we need to talk about some major parts of speech.

Adjectives

Adjectives are a huge part of speaking any language. They allow you to describe nouns and objects. French adjectives are relatively easy for the most part. However, their only tricky asset is that the vast majority of them have to match their respective objects which they describe in terms of plurality and gender. This can make for quite a mess when you're newer to French.

Take, for example, the French adjective *joli*, meaning "pretty" or "cute". If I wanted to say "He is pretty", I would say "Il est joli". However, if I wanted to say "she is pretty", I would instead say "Elle est joli*e*". Notice the addition of the *e* to make it feminine.

Depending upon what exactly the adjective is, there are different ways to make one feminine. For example, the vast majority of adjectives can be made feminine simply by the addition of an *-e* to the end of it.

A key difference between English and French adjectives is that French adjectives nearly always go *after* the noun in question, which can really trip you up at first. After a while, it starts to make sense in its own way - after all, it's just another manner of communication. However, avoid falling into the trap of accidentally using an adjective incorrectly because you don't know any better.

Some adjectives *do* go before the noun though. It can be hard to remember which ones exactly, but just think of the following acronym: *beauty, age, goodness, size*. Adjectives which have to do with those typically can go before the adjective rather than after.

Additionally, you very much need to be wary of the meanings of your adjectives. Certain adjectives can go before *and* after a noun. However, this can create two diametrically different meanings depending upon the placement. Take, for example, *curieux*.

If you place *curieux* before the noun, it means weird or strange. However, if you place it after the noun, it means curious or inquisitive. In other words, the correct adjective placement can be the difference between giving praise to your kid and calling them a total weirdo. Be more careful than to call your kid a total weirdo, my friend.

Adverbs

Adverbs describe verbs and adjectives. Adverbs are incredibly easy to form. You may notice a parallel between French adverbs and Spanish adverbs if you've spent any time study Spanish, by chance: you form adverbs by taking the adjective you'd like to make into an adverb, putting it into its feminine form, and appending *ment* to it, similar to how you form adverbs in Spanish.

Take, for example, the adjective *lent*, meaning slow. Now, let's put it in its feminine form, which gives us *lente*. Then, we just add *ment*, the French equivalent of the English "-ly", and we've got *lentement* meaning *slowly*. In a sentence:

"Parleriez-vous lentement? Je ne parle pas bien français." ("Would you speak slowly? I don't speak French well.")

Overall, the process of creating adverbs in French is super easy.

Conjunctions

Conjunctions are an integral part of any language. I say this because we haven't talked about them at all, yet there's not really a part of language which is dedicated to providing logical order to sentences so much as the conjunctions are.

There are quite a few conjunctions in the French language. More than quite a few, actually. There are a ton of them. Let's start with the coordinating conjunctions. What coordinating conjunctions are are conjunctions that serve to connect two different clauses without placing some sort of emphasis on one or the other. In French, there are actually seven different coordinating conjunctions.

Mais - but
Et - and
Ou - or
Or - now
Ni - neither, nor (used in pairs)
Parce que - because
Donc - thus, so

These all have their own particular uses, and you can likely figure out approximately how to use them based off of their English translations. Indeed, basing their usage off of their English translations is a relatively safe way to use these powerful parts of speech.

Next, there are *subordinating* conjunctions. These are a bit more complicated to use, so if something a little weird, I'll put an example by it in parentheses.

Comme - like, as, since (*Il est courageux comme le léon - he is courageous like the lion*)

Quand - when
Lorsque - when
Que - that (*Je sais bien que tu as raison - I know for certain that you're right.*)
Si - if

And then there are just some general ones that you need to know:

Avant que - before the event of (*Je suis parti avant qu'elle est arrivée. - I left before she arrived.*)
Autant que - to the extent that
Bien que - although
Tel(le)(s) que - such that

This is just scratching the surface, really. There are absurd amounts of French conjunctions out there. But with the knowledge that I've given you thus far, you should be able to make your way around moderately well.

Prepositions

We've already learned a couple of prepositions in French, such as à (meaning to, at, or in) and de (meaning of or from). However, there are even more that we haven't talked about! A lot of these things which have relatively direct English translations, but others are ones which will take a bit more explanation. Let's dive in.

à cause de - thanks to (negative)
à travers - through
après - after
au lieu de - instead of something
avant - before
avec - with
chez - *chez* is a tricky one. It can mean "at the location of *x* person's house", where chez moi means "at my home"or "to my home"; it can also mean "at a company's name" as in "J'ai mangé chez McDonald's"; lastly, it can simply mean "for" - "Quel marche chez toi?" meaning "What worked for you?"
contre - against something
dans - in (used if followed by article)
depuis - since, for (in reference to a length of time)
dès - ever since
en - in (used if not followed by article)
entre - between
environ - approximately
grâce à - thanks to (positive)
jusqu'à - up to, until
par - by, before, alongside, through
pendant - during, for (in reference to a length of time)

pour - for
sous - under
sur - on
vers - towards something, but also to say "around" when talking about
numbers

Those are a ton of prepositions to hopefully get you started. You need to be
using a lot of this to the extent that you can. Be writing to yourself in private
journals and things of the like; try your hand at reading online news and forums.
Work with what you've learned.

Chapter 6: Conversational Necessities

So you've landed in France or Quebec and wherever, and you've got a working knowledge of the *mechanics* of French. But *oupsie*, you've got no clue how to have a conversation. What do we do here?

Well, I'll admit, I waited until the last chapter to teach you to have a French conversation because otherwise, you'd just be doing the tourist-y thing of learning several words and phrases without learning *how* they work or *why* they work. And I'll be honest, you'll have a much easier time communicating in France or Quebec if you know how the language works, because the tourist-y phrases hardly make any sense from a linguistic standpoint.

Anyhow, I'll walk you through a French conversation, perhaps with an acquaintance or perhaps with someone new.

The first thing you're going to want to do, of course, is say hello. There are a lot of ways that you can do this in French.

First, if it's in the morning or afternoon, you could say *bonjour*. If it's the evening, you could say *bonsoir*.

This is very formal though. In less formal situations, perhaps around people you know, say *Salut!* instead. (sah-loo) You could also get away with saying *Hé!*

And of course, if you're answering the phone, you say *Allô*. (ah-loh) This is equivalent to the English "hello?" on the phone, and carries the same weight.

If you're wanting to welcome people, you'd say "Bienvenue!". (bee-ahn-vuu-noo)

Anyhow, now you've said hello. What do you do?

Well, you could ask the person a little bit about how they're doing. If they're a stranger, your best bet is to say "Comment allez-vous?" which means "How are you doing?" It's the formal phrase, and can be used with strangers as well as the elderly and your higher-ups in school and work. If you know the person a bit better, you might say "Comment ça va?" (coh-mohn sah vah) or "Comment vas-tu?" (coh-mohn vah tue)

Let's say that you want to get to know them. You may say "Qu'est-ce que tu aimes faire?" or "qu'est-ce que vous aimez faire?" depending upon the formality of the situation, both meaning "What do you like to do?"

Or maybe you're younger and trying to find out how old someone about your age is. In that case, you could just say "Tu as quel âge?", literally meaning

"You have what age?"

Finally, it's going to eventually come to be time to end the conversation, sadly. At that point, there are a couple different ways in which you could say goodbye.

The first is ***au revoir***, meaning simply "until we meet again". Pronounced oh ruu-vwah, it's useful in most any situation, formal or informal.

Then, there is **à plus tard** (ah plue tar) which means "see you later", but this is purely informal. You may hear this as "à plus" (ah plues).

Next up is **à bientôt** (ah bee-ehn-toh) which means "see you soon". You can use this formally, as well as informally.

Also useful is **à la prochaine** (ah lah pro-shehn), which means "until next time". Use this when you don't know when you're going to see the other person.

À demain (ah duu-mahn) can mean "see you tomorrow".

Last is **adieu**, which is the most final goodbye. You only use this when you know you'll never see somebody again. If the French hit one nail on the head every time, it's dramaticism.

To spare you from the cheesy explanations from everything, I'm now just going to put some really useful phrases that you're probably going to end up using at one time or another in your journey. I hope the context and background I've given you serves you well in understanding them and there usage:

S'il te plaît/s'il vous plaît - *Please.*
Je voudrais [...] - *I would like [...]*
Je prends [...] - *I'll have [...]*
Merci. - *Thank you.*
Je m'appelle [...] - *My name is [...]*
Comment est [...] - *How is the [...] ? / What's [...] like?*
D'accord. - *Okay.*
Je ne sais pas. - *I don't know.*
Je n'ai aucune idée. - *I have no idea.*
De rien. - *You're welcome.*
Pas de problème. - *No problem.*
Pas de soucis. - *Don't worry.*
Je ne te comprends pas. - *I'm not understanding you.*
Comment dit-on [...] en français? - *How do you say [...] in French?*
Qu'est-ce que ça va dire, [...] ? - *What does [...] mean?*
Combien coûte-t-il? - *How much does it cost?*

Conclusion

Thank for making it through to the end of **TITLE** let's hope it was informative and able to provide you with all of the tools you need to achieve your goals whatever they may be.

The next step is to go further with all of this. I've given you the essential grammatical knowledge, but the trade-off of teaching you so much so briskly is that I didn't give you as much in-depth knowledge regarding vocabulary as I would have liked to. This works out in your favor, though - I encourage you to use Duolingo in order to build your vocabulary. This is because where free online services fail is where I've succeeded. I've tried to give you a firm *grammatical* basis of French, that way when you do learn vocab, you know precisely how to use it. Duolingo and services as such are great for memorizing vocab, but don't do so hot when it comes to giving you the practical knowledge of application.

By using the combination of the two - my technical knowledge of the language and the great reference book I've left you with, and the immense focus of Duolingo on vocabulary, you'll be set straight for success and will have an awe-inspiring grasp of the language in no time.

You can also use the site ankisrs.net in order to put the vocab that you've learned into flash cards. You can use this online flash cards utility in order to hone your ability to speak French like a champion.

I genuinely hope that over the course of this book, I've managed to set you up for success. I fully believe that I have, but the proof will be in the pudding of you learning and applying French in your day to day life. I fully expect that you can do that.

Finally, if you found this book useful in anyway, a review on Amazon is always appreciated!

Enjoy yourself, and every second that you spend learning this beautiful language.

Help me improve this book

While I have never met you, if you made it through this book I know that you are the kind of person that is wanting to get better and is willing to take on tough feedback to get to that point. You and I are cut from the same cloth in that respect. I am always looking to get better and I wish to not just improve myself, but also this book. If you have positive feedback, please take the time to leave a review. It will help other find this book and it can help change a life in the same way that it changed yours. If you have constructive feedback, please also leave a review. It will help me better understand what you, the reader, need to make significant improvements in your life. I will take your feedback and use it to improve this book so that it can become more powerful and beneficial to all those who encounter it.

REMEMBER TO JOIN THE GROUP NOW!

If you have not joined the Mastermind Self Development group yet, now is your time! You will receive videos and articles from top authorities in self development as well as a special group only offers on new books and training programs. There will also be a monthly member only draw that gives you a chance to win any book from your Kindle wish list!

If you sign up through this link http://www.mastermindselfdevelopment.com/specialreport you will also get a special free report on the Wheel of Life. This report will give you a visual look at your current life and then take you through a series of exercises that will help you plan what your perfect life looks like. The workbook does not end there; we then take you through a process to help you plan how to achieve that perfect life. The process is very powerful and has the potential to change your life forever. Join the group now and start to change your life! http://www.mastermindselfdevelopment.com/specialreport

You will also love these other great titles from Mastermind Self Development!

You will want to check out these other great titles Mastermind Self Development. All available in the Kindle store or you can just click on covers below.

http://viewbook.at/selflove

http://mybook.to/mindfulnesssecrets

You can also find these titles by searching them in the Kindle store on Amazon.

LEARN FRENCH

Short Stories for Beginners to Learn French Quickly and Easily

Free membership into the Mastermind Self Development Group!

For a limited time, you can join the Mastermind Self Development Group for free! You will receive videos and articles from top authorities in self development as well as a special group only offers on new books and training programs. There will also be a monthly member only draw that gives you a chance to win any book from your Kindle wish list!

If you sign up through this link http://www.mastermindselfdevelopment.com/specialreport you will also get a special free report on the Wheel of Life. This report will give you a visual look at your current life and then take you through a series of exercises that will help you plan what your perfect life looks like. The workbook does not end there; we then take you through a process to help you plan how to achieve that perfect life. The process is very powerful and has the potential to change your life forever. Join the group now and start to change your life!
http://www.mastermindselfdevelopment.com/specialreport

Table of Contents

Introduction

Congratulations on downloading this book, and thank you for doing so! Or, should I say, *Félicitations d'avoir téléchargé ce livre et merci de l'avoir fait!*

Welcome to a book that will help you to advance your French language abilities! To learn any language, you need a basis of grammar and vocabulary. But when it comes to actually communicating in your new language, memorizing flash cards and grammar rules just won't cut it. In this book, you will learn the basics of French and hopefully be able to put your knowledge into context. That's where this book comes in! Five fun, unique short stories in French will challenge your vocabulary and comprehension—but don't worry, the English version is always at your fingertips. Each chapter begins with the French version of the story. Within the French text, vocabulary words are identified with italics. The English version is next, and all chapters end with a list of key vocabulary words and several questions (in French) to test your understanding and your grammar. If you want to answer the questions before reading the English version, skip over to the questions section. Answers to the vocabulary, grammar, and comprehension questions can be found in the Answers chapter at the end of the book.

As you are reading, also keep an eye out for the asterisk (*) symbol. These asterisks will identify cultural elements of the stories. Understanding these cultural notes will help your French comprehension abilities. Learning a language, after all, is also about becoming familiar with another culture. By practicing your French, you will grow your understanding of French culture. Explanations for passages marked with an asterisk can be found at the end of each chapter, following the question section.

The first four stories in this book are written mostly in the present tense. There are only a few verbs in past or future tense used. Usually, when you first start learning a language, you begin with the present tense only. However, to really expand your French abilities, you will also need to use other tenses. For this reason, the final story in this book is written mostly in the past tense. If you are not used to practicing the past tense, you might find this story to be more difficult. If you are comfortable with the present tense and want a challenge, the fifth story is a great introduction to using the past tense in everyday situations.

By reading stories in French and using vocabulary in context, you will be able to get a sense of the syntax and flow of French. The English and French syntaxes are not the same, and it can be a real challenge to memorize the exact grammar rules for each type of sentence. Learning French through short stories allows you to bypass this time-consuming step and simply get a feel for how French sentences are constructed. In addition, it's always easier to remember new words if you can put them in context right away! I want learning French to be as easy and fun for you as possible, and I hope you enjoy these stories and the benefits they bring to your French abilities!

A final bit of advice before you begin this book: over the years, I have found www.wordreference.com to be an invaluable resource for looking up French vocabulary and grammar. Maybe you will find it useful as well!

Chapter 1: La Famille de Manon/Manon's Family

La Famille de Manon

Manon a dix-sept ans et elle *a* une grande *famille.*

Manon habite dans une maison avec sa *mère*, Sylvie, son *père*, Paul, et son petit *frère*, Simon. Sylvie et Paul ont quarante-neuf ans. Simon a treize ans. Manon a deux *soeurs* et un autre frère, mais ils sont plus âgés. Ses soeurs *vont* à l'université et son frère est *marié.**

Les soeurs de Manon *s'appellent* Camille et Eugénie. Camille a dix-neuf ans. Elle *étudie* les sciences à l'université. Elle veut devenir *médecin.* Eugénie étudie l'anglais parce qu'elle *veut devenir* professeur d'anglais. Elle a vingt-deux ans.

Le grand frère de Manon a vingt-cinq ans et il s'appelle Vincent. Vincent est marié avec une jolie *femme* qui s'appelle Agnès. Ils habite dans la même ville que Manon et ses parents. Vincent et Agnès ont deux *enfants.* Leur *fille*, Tiphaine, a deux ans et leur *fils*, Jérôme, a cinq mois. Vincent est *dentiste* et Agnès est *banquière.*

Manon aime bien sa *nièce* et son *neveu.* Quand Vincent et Agnès *sont occupés*, elle va souvent à leur maison pour voir Tiphaine et Jérôme. Elle pense qu'elle veut travailler dans *un crèche* quand elle est plus âgée.

Les grands-parents de Manon habitent dans un petit village. Le dimanche, Manon visite ses grands-parents avec ses parents et Simon. Quand Camille et Eugénie ne sont pas trop occupées, elles visitent leurs grands-parents aussi. Manon aime visiter ses grands-parents. Sa *grande-mère* prépare *un repas* et toute la famille mange beaucoup. Son *grand-père* aime des *jeux de cartes* et il joue avec Manon. *De temps en temps*, ils vont à *la pâtisserie* pour acheter des *gâteaux.* Simon mange beaucoup de gâteaux !

Manon est très contente d'avoir une grande famille !

Manon's Family

Manon is seventeen years old, and she has a big family.

Manon lives in a house with her mother, Sylvie, her father, Paul, and her little brother, Simon. Sylvie and Paul are forty-nine years old. Simon is thirteen years old. Manon has two sisters and one other brother, but they are older. Her sisters go to the university and her brother is married.

Manon's sisters are named Camille and Eugénie. Camille is nineteen years old. She studies science at the university. She wants to become a doctor. Eugénie studies English because she wants to become an English teacher. She is twenty-two years old.

Manon's big brother is twenty-five years old, and his name is Vincent. Vincent is married to a pretty woman named Agnès. They live in the same city as Manon and her parents. Vincent and Agnès have two children. Their daughter, Tiphaine, is two years old and their son, Jérôme, is five months old. Vincent is a dentist, and Agnès is a banker.

Manon really likes her niece and nephew. When Vincent and Agnès are busy, she often goes to their house to see Tiphaine and Jérôme. She thinks she wants to work in a daycare when she is older.

Manon's grandparents live in a small town. On Sundays, Manon visits her grandparents with her parents and Simon. When Camille and Eugénie aren't too busy, they visit their grandparents too. Manon likes to visit her grandparents. Her grandmother prepares a meal, and the whole family eats a lot. Her grandfather likes card games, and he plays with Manon. Sometimes, they go to the pastry shop to buy cakes. Simon eats a lot of cakes!

Manon is very happy to have a big family!

Vocabulary, Grammar, and Comprehension Questions

<u>Nouns</u>

Le banquier/La banquière (nmf) = the banker

Le/La dentiste (nmf) = the dentist

L'enfant (nm) = the child

La famille (nf) = the family

La femme (nf) = the woman, the wife

La fille (nf) = the girl, the daughter

Le fils (nm) = the son

Le frère (nm) = the brother

Le gâteau (nm) = the cake

La grande-mère (nf) = the grandmother

Les grands-parents (np) = the grandparents

Le grand-père (nm) = the grandfather

Le jeu de cartes (nm) = the card game

Le médecin (nm) = the doctor

La mère (nf) = the mother

Le neveu (nm) = the nephew

La nièce (nf) = the niece

La pâtisserie = the pastry shop, the pastry

Le père (nm) = the father

Le repas (nm) = the meal

La soeur (nf) = the sister

<u>Adjectives</u>

Marié(e)(s) = married

Occupé(e)(s) = busy

<u>Verbs</u>

Aller = to go

S'appeler = to be called, to be named (reflexive verb)

Avoir = to have

Devenir = to become

Être = to be

Etudier = to study

Vouloir = to want

<u>Useful Expressions</u>

De temps en temps = sometimes

<u>Questions</u>

Répondez aux questions:

1. Comment s'appellent les soeurs de Manon ?
2. Quand est-ce que Manon visite ses grands-parents ?
3. Quel âge a Simon ?
4. Qu'est-ce qu'Eugénie étudie à l'université ?
5. Manon a combien de nieces ?

Remplissez les blancs dans le texte avec le mot qui convient:

frère	famille	enfants	s'appelle
marié	soeurs	parents	université

Manon habite avec ses ___________ et son _________. Ses deux __________ étudient à l'_______________. Son frère Vincent est _________. Sa femme __________ Agnès. Ils ont deux __________. Manon aime sa grande __________.

Conjuguez les verbes:

1. Avoir

J'	Nous
Tu	Vous
Il/Elle/On	Ils/Elles

2. Être

Je	Nous

Tu	Vous
Il/Elle/On	Ils/Elles

3. Aller

Je	Nous
Tu	Vous
Il/Elle/On	Ils/Elles

4. Vouloir

Je	Nous
Tu	Vous
Il/Elle/On	Ils/Elles

Answers in the back of book

*Legal marriage in France is completely secular. Couples must be married by an official in the municipality where they or their parents live. Couples who practice a religion often have a religious marriage ceremony in addition to this civil ceremony, but the religious ceremony on its own does not have legal standing. France also has a form of civil union known as a *Pacte civil de solidarité*, or *PACS*, which was created in 1999. Two adults of the same or different genders can get *pacsé*, and this gives them tax and financial advantages similar to those of married couples. *PACS* was a precursor to gay marriage in France, which became legal in 2013.

Chapter 2: Un Grand Jour/A Big Day

Un Grand Jour

Axelle *se lève tôt* le matin. C'est jeudi ! Finalement ! Elle *saut* du lit et descend l'escalier.

«Maman ! Papa ! C'est jeudi !»

«Je sais, ma chérie, répond sa maman. Je vois que tu es très enthousiaste ce matin !»

«Oui, oui, répond Axelle. Et toi, Maman, tu *sais* pourquoi !»

«Oui, pour sûr, dit Maman. Mais il faut quand même prendre *le petit déjeuner* et aller à l'école.»

Axelle *prend* son petit déjeuner. Elle mange des tranches de *pain* avec de la *confiture*. Elle boit du *chocolat chaud* avec du *lait*. Après le petit déjeuner, elle *se brosse* les dents. Elle s'habille dans sa *robe préférée*. C'est quand même un grand jour ! Il faut être joli.

Axelle et Maman prennent le métro pour aller à l'école. Le matin, le métro est *comblé*. Axelle dit bonjour à *tout le monde*.

«Bonjour, Monsieur Durand ! *Comment allez-vous ?*»

«Bonjour, Mademoiselle Axelle, répond Monsieur Durand. Je vais bien, merci beaucoup. J'aime bien ta robe.»

«Merci, Monsieur Durand, dit Axelle. C'est ma robe préférée.»

«Mais bien sûr ! dit Monsieur Durand. Aujourd'hui c'est jeudi ! C'est un grand jour pour toi.»

«Oui, répond Axelle. Mais je *dois* quand même aller à l'école !»

«Oui, l'école est très importante,» dit Monsieur Durand.

Après dix minutes, ils arrivent à l'arrêt. Axelle et Maman descendent du métro et montent l'escalier jusqu'à la rue. Ils *traversent* la rue pour arriver à l'école primaire et disent bonjour à *l'institutrice.*

«Bonjour, Maîtresse ! dit Axelle. Aujourd'hui c'est un jour important !»

«Je le sais bien, Axelle. Je *vois* que tu porte une jolie robe ce matin» répond l'institutrice.

«Oui ! dit Axelle. Je porte ma robe préférée parce que c'est un grand jour.»

«Très bien, Axelle, répond l'institutrice. Mais il faut attendre la fin de la journée.»

Axelle dit au revoir à sa maman et rentre dans l'école primaire. Elle est en CE1*. Dans la salle de classe, elle dit bonjour à ses copines :

«Salut, Jade ! Salut, Isabelle ! *Ça va ?*»

«Salut, Axelle ! répondent Jade et Isabelle. *Ça va très bien*. Aujourd'hui c'est le grand jour, n'est-ce pas ?»

«Oui, c'est aujourd'hui ! dit Axelle. Mais je dois attendre la fin de la journée.»

L'institutrice arrive dans la salle de classe.

«Bonjour, tout le monde !» dit-elle.

«Bonjour, Maîtresse !» répond la classe.

La journée commence avec des maths. *Ensuite*, les élèves *font* le français et l'art. Dans le cours d'art, Axelle fait *un dessin* de sa famille. Il y a trois membres de la famille: sa mère, son père, et Axelle. Sa mère est *petite* et *brune*. Son père est *grand* et *blond*. Axelle est petite et blonde. A midi, tous les élèves mangent *le déjeuner*. Ils mangent tous ensemble à *la cantine*. Aujourd'hui il y a *une soupe* à l'oignon, du *pain*, des *haricots verts*, et des *yaourts* pour *le dessert*. Axelle aime bien manger le déjeuner dans la cantine. Après le déjeuner, elle sort dans *le cour de récréation* avec ses copines, Jade et Isabelle. Elles *jouent* à *cache-cache* et s'amusent bien. Il fait beau et Axelle, Jade, et Isabelle ne *voulaient* pas rentrer dans le bâtiment.

«Allez, les enfants ! dit l'institutrice. On va commencer le cours de musique !»

Dans le cours de musique, les élèves chantent tous ensemble. L'institutrice joue du piano. Axelle préfère le cours d'art, mais elle aime écouter de la musique. Elle écoute *souvent* des *chansons* en anglais. Elle veut bien apprendre l'anglais. Les cours d'anglais commencent l'année *prochaine*, en CE2, mais Axelle sait *déjà* dire "Hello!"

Après le cours de musique, il y a un cours d'histoire et un cours de science. Axelle attend la fin de la journée avec impatience. Finalement, les cours sont finis.

«*A demain*, tout le monde !» dit l'institutrice.

«A demain, Maîtresse !» répond la classe.

Axelle sort de l'école. *D'habitude*, elle attend sa maman et elles prennent le métro ensemble pour revenir à la maison, mais aujourd'hui tout est différent. Maman et Papa attendent Axelle dans *la voiture*.

«Salut, Axelle ! dit Papa. Ça va bien ?»

«Oui ! dit Axelle. Il y avait un cours d'art aujourd'hui et j'ai fait un dessin !»

«C'est très joli, dit Papa. Maintenant, est-ce que tu es *prête* ?»

«Oui, Papa ! répond Axelle. Je suis prête !»

Maman *conduit* la voiture et après quinze minutes la famille arrive au *magasin*. Axelle *sourit*. Elle a attendu toute la journée, mais maintenant elle peut choisir le quatrième membre de la famille.

Axelle, sa mère, et son père entrent dans *le magasin*. Là, derrière *la fenêtre*, il y a des *chatons*: un chaton noir, un chaton orange, un chaton gris, et un chaton blanc.

«Tu peux choisir, Axelle,» disent ses parents.

Axelle regarde les quatres chatons. Le chaton noir et le chaton gris dorment. Le chaton blanc joue avec *un ballon*. Le chaton orange regarde Axelle.

«Je pense... Je pense que je veux le chaton orange,» dit Axelle.

«Très bien !» disent ses parents.

Le vendeur ramasse le chaton orange. Axelle prend le chaton dans ses bras.

«Bonjour, petit chaton ! dit-elle. Je t'appelle Loulou»

«Miaou !» dit le chaton.

Axelle est très contente. Ses parents sourient. C'est la fin d'un grand jour.

You are halfway done!

Congratulations on making it to the halfway point of the journey. Many try and give up long before even getting to this point, so you are to be congratulated on this. You have shown that you are serious about getting better every day. I am also serious about improving my life, and helping others get better along the way. To do this I need your feedback. Click on the link below and take a moment to let me know how this book has helped you. If you feel there is something missing or something you would like to see differently, I would love to know about it. I want to ensure that as you and I improve, this book continues to improve as well. Thank you for taking the time to ensure that we are all getting the most from each other.

A Big Day

Axelle gets up early in the morning. It's Thursday! Finally! She leaps out of bed and goes down the stairs.

"Mom! Dad! It's Thursday!"

"I know, dear," replied her mom. "I can see that you're very excited this morning!"

"Yes, yes," replied Axelle. "And you know why, Mom!"

"Yes, of course," said Mom. "But you still have to eat breakfast and go to school."

Axelle has her breakfast. She eats slices of bread with jam. She drinks hot chocolate with milk. After breakfast, she brushes her teeth. She puts on her favorite dress. It is, after all, a big day! It's good to look pretty.

Axelle and Mom take the subway to get to school. In the morning, the subway is full. Axelle says hello to everyone.

"Hello, Mr. Durand! How are you?"

"Hello, Miss Axelle," replies Mr. Durand. "I'm doing well, thank you. I really like your dress."

"Thank you, Mr. Durand," says Axelle. "It's my favorite dress."

"But of course!" says Mr. Durand. "Today is Thursday! It's a big day for you."

"Yes," replies Axelle. "But I still have to go to school!"

"Yes, school is very important," says Mr. Durand.

After ten minutes, they arrive at the stop. Axelle and Mom get off the subway and climb the stairs up to the street. They cross the street to get to the elementary school and say hello to the teacher.

"Hello, teacher!" says Axelle. "Today is an important day!"

"I know, Axelle. I see that you're wearing a pretty dress this morning," says the teacher.

"Yes!" says Axelle. "I'm wearing my favorite dress because it's a big day."

"Very good, Axelle," replies the teacher. "But you'll have to wait to the end of the day."

Axelle says goodbye to her mom and goes into the elementary school. She is in first grade. In the classroom, she says hello to her friends:

"Hi, Jade! Hi, Isabelle! How are you?"

"Hi, Axelle!" reply Jade and Isabelle. "We're doing great. Today is the big day, isn't it?"

"Yes, it's today!" says Axelle. "But I have to wait until the end of the day."

The teacher arrives in the classroom.

"Hello, everyone!" she says.

"Hello, teacher!" replies the class.

The day starts with math. Next, the students do French and art. In the art class, Axelle does a drawing of her family. There are three members of the family: her mother, her father, and Axelle. Her mother is short and has brown hair. Her father is tall and blonde. Axelle is short and blonde. At noon, all of the students eat lunch. They all eat together in the cafeteria. Today there is a French onion soup, bread, green beans, and yogurt for dessert. Axelle likes eating lunch in the cafeteria a lot. After lunch, she goes out to the playground with her friends, Jade and Isabelle. They play hide-and-seek and have lots of fun. It is nice outside, and Axelle, Jade, and Isabelle don't want to back into the building.

"Come along, children!" says the teacher. "We are going to start the music class!"

In the music class, the students sing all together. The teacher plays the piano. Axelle prefers the art class, but she likes listening to music. She often listens to songs in English. She really wants to learn English. The English classes start the next year, in second grade, but Axelle already knows how to say "Hello!"

After the music class, there is a history class and a science class. Axelle waits impatiently for the end of the day. Finally, the classes are finished.

"See you tomorrow, everyone!" says the teacher.

"See you tomorrow, teacher!" says the class.

Axelle leaves the school. Usually, she waits for her mom and they take the subway together to get back home, but today everything is different. Mom and Dad are waiting for Axelle in the car.

"Hi, Axelle!" says Dad. "Are things going well?"

"Yes!" says Axelle. "There was an art class today, and I made a drawing!"

“It’s very pretty,” says Dad. “Now, are you ready?”

“Yes, Dad!” replies Axelle. “I’m ready!”

Mom drives the car, and after fifteen minutes the family arrives at the store. Axelle smiles. She has waited all day, but now she can choose the fourth member of the family.

Axelle, her mother, and her father go into the store. There, behind the window, are kittens: a black kitten, an orange kitten, a gray kitten, and a white kitten.

“You can choose, Axelle,” say her parents.

Axelle looks at the four kittens. The black kitten and the gray kitten are sleeping. The white kitten is playing with a ball. The orange kitten looks at Axelle.

“I think... I think I want the orange kitten,” says Axelle.

“Very good!” say her parents.

The salesman picks up the orange kitten. Axelle takes it in her arms.

“Hello, little kitten!” she says. “I’m going to call you Loulou.”

“Meow!” says the kitten.

Axelle is very happy. Her parents smile. It’s the end of a big day.

Vocabulary, Grammar, and Comprehension Questions

<u>Nouns</u>

Le ballon (nm) = the ball

La cantine (nf) = the cafeteria

La chanson (nf) = the song

Le chaton (nm) = the kitten

Le chocolat chaud (nm) = the hot chocolate

La confiture (nf) = the jam

Le cour de récréation (nm) = the playground at a school

Le déjeuner (nm) = lunch

Le dessert (nm) = the dessert

Le dessin (nm) = the drawing

La fenêtre (nf) = the window

Les haricots verts (np) = the green beans, no liaison between *les* and *haricots*

Le lait (nm) = the milk

L'institutrice (nf) = the elementary school teacher

Le magasin (nm) = the store

Le pain (nm) = the bread

Le petit déjeuner (nm) = the breakfast

La robe (nf) = the dress

La soupe (nf) = the soup

Le vendeur (nm) = the salesman. Also "la vendeuse" (nf), the saleswoman.

La voiture (nf) = the car

Le yaourt (nm) = the yogurt

<u>Adjectives</u>

Blond(e)(s) = blonde, having blonde hair

Brun(e)(s) = having brown hair

Comblé(e)(s) = full, as in a train car or room (does not describe having eaten a lot)

Grand(e)(s) = big, tall

Petit(e)(s) = small, short, little

Préféré(e)(s) = favorite, preferred

Prêt(e)(s) = ready

Prochain(e)(s) = next

Adverbs

Déjà = already

D'habitude = usually

Ensuite = next, afterwards

Souvent = often

Tôt = early

Verbs

Se brosser = to brush (reflexive verb)

Conduire = to drive

Devoir = to have to

Faire = to make/to do

Jouer = to play

(Se) lever = to get up (reflexive verb), to lift

Prendre = to take

Ramasser = to collect, to pick up

Sauter = to jump

Savoir = to know (facts)

Sourire = to smile

Traverser = to cross

Voir = to see

<u>Useful Expressions</u>

A demain ! = See you tomorrow!

Ça va? = How are you?/How's it going? Informal way of speaking.

Ça va bien/mal = It's going good/bad. The response "Ça va" can also be used alone to indicate that things are going fine.

Cache-cache = hide-and-seek, the children's game

Comment allez-vous? = How are you? Formal way of speaking.

Tout le monde = everyone, frequently used to address groups of people

<u>Questions</u>

Répondez aux questions:

1. Qu'est-ce qu'Axelle porte ?
2. Axelle fait un dessin à l'école. Qu'est-ce qu'elle dessine ?
3. Pourquoi est-ce que c'est un grand jour pour Axelle ?
4. Quel est le nom du chaton d'Axelle ?

Remplissez les blancs dans le texte. Il faut s'accorder les noms et les adjectifs.

1. Axelle est une ______________ (petit) fille.
2. Axelle et son père sont ______________ (blond).
3. Aujourd'hui, le métro est ______________ (comblé).
4. Les institutrices sont ______________ (grand).

Conjuguez les verbes:

1. Faire

Je	Nous
Tu	Vous
Il/Elle/On	Ils/Elles

2. Jouer

Je	Nous
Tu	Vous
Il/Elle/On	Ils/Elles

3. Savoir

Je	Nous
Tu	Vous
Il/Elle/On	Ils/Elles

4. Voir

Je	Nous
Tu	Vous
Il/Elle/On	Ils/Elles

Answers in the back of book

*Axelle is in grade *CE1* in school. The French school system is organized differently than the American school system. Elementary school, or *école primaire*, has five levels:

Cours préparatoire (CP) = ages 6–7, corresponding to first grade

Cours élémentaire 1 (CE1) = ages 7–8, corresponding to second grade

Cours élémentaire 2 (CE2) = ages 8–9, corresponding to third grade

Cours moyen 1 (CM1) = ages 9–10, corresponding to fourth grade

Cours moyen 2 (CM2) = ages 10–11, corresponding to fifth grade

Students then go to middle school, or *collège*, which has four levels:

6ème = ages 11–12, corresponding to sixth grade

5ème = ages 12–13, corresponding to seventh grade

4ème = ages 13–14, corresponding to eighth grade

3ème = ages 14–15, corresponding to ninth grade or freshman year

At the end of *collège*, students take the *brevet*, a comprehensive exam. If they are sixteen years old and pass the *brevet*, they are allowed to leave school, but most students do not. They continue to the high school level, or *lycée*, which takes three years.

Seconde = ages 15–16, corresponding to tenth grade or sophomore year

Première = ages 16–17, corresponding to eleventh grade or junior year

Terminale = ages 17–18, corresponding to twelfth grade or senior year

French high school students start to specialize in certain subjects at *lycée*, unlike American students. At the end of the three years, they take the *Baccalaureat* (usually shortened to *le bac*). Passing *le bac* means they have achieved the equivalent of the American high school diploma. *Le bac* is also the entrance exam for most of France's universities.

Chapter 3: Un Voyage/A Trip

Un Voyage

L'avion arrive à l'Aéroport Roissy-Charles de Gaulle vers 10h du matin. Katie *regarde* l'aéroport par la fenêtre de l'avion. Elle est en France !

Katie *rêvait depuis longtemps* d'un voyage en France. Cette année, elle a finalement eu l'opportunité de *partir à l'étranger*. Elle visite Paris avec sa mère, son père, et sa *meilleure* amie, Amy. Katie et Amy ont seize ans et elles aime bien l'histoire. Elles veulent *apprendre* l'histoire de Paris pendant ce voyage.

Katie et sa mère ont trouvé *un hôtel* chic en centre-ville. Pour arriver à l'hôtel, ils *ont besoin de* prendre le RER*. Katie demande à un monsieur comment *acheter* des billets.

«*Excusez-moi*, monsieur. Comment est-ce que j'achète des billets de RER ?»

«Ce n'est pas difficile, mademoiselle, répond le monsieur. Vous *pouvez* acheter des billets là bas. *Il faut* demander à la dame derrière la fenêtre.»

«*Merci beaucoup*, monsieur,» dit Katie.

«Je vous conseil d'acheter des tickets de métro en même temps, dit le monsieur. C'est plus *facile*. Vous pouvez acheter *un carnet* de dix tickets et ça coûte moins cher.»

«Merci ! répond Katie. Je vais faire ça.»

Elle achète de la dame quatre billets de RER et un carnet de tickets de métro.

«Ça coûte combien ?» demande Katie.

«Ça coûte €54.50» réponde la dame.

Katie pense que c'est *cher*, mais elle sait que les vacances à Paris coûtent beaucoup. Elle *donne* €60 à la dame.

Katie, sa mère, son père, et Amy *montent* dans le RER en direction de Paris. Le voyage prend cinquante minutes. Katie et Amy sont très *fatiguées* après le long voyage en avion et elles dorment un peu. Eventuellement le petit groupe arrive à l'hôtel. Katie *partage une chambre* avec Amy et ses parents partagent une deuxième chambre.

«J'ai besoin de faire *la sieste*,» dit le père de Katie.

«Moi aussi,» dit Amy.

Tous les quatre *décident* de faire la sieste. Après une heure, il descendent pour voir le *quartier*.

«Oh ! Je peux voir la Tour Eiffel !» dit Katie.

«Moi aussi ! dit Amy. Ce n'est pas *loin*. Est-ce qu'on peut visiter la Tour Eiffel ce *soir* ?»

«*Pourquoi pas ?* disent les parents de Katie. On va dîner dans un restaurant et après on peut visiter la Tour Eiffel.»

Ils trouvent un *joli* petit restaurant près de l'hôtel. Le restaurant sert des plats *traditionnels* français. Katie et son père mangent un bon boeuf bourguignon. Sa mère prend une salade niçoise. Amy est très *aventureuse* et elle prend des escargots. La mère et le père de Katie boivent aussi un bon *vin* français.

Après le dîner, ils marchent tous vers la Tour Eiffel. Katie achète quatre billets pour monter jusqu'au *sommet* de la tour. Ils décident de prendre *l'ascenseur* parce qu'ils ne veulent pas monter 1.710 marches !

C'était une bonne idée de visiter la Tour Eiffel le soir. Quand ils arrivent au sommet, le soleil se couche et le ciel est orange, rose, et violet. Amy, Katie, et ses parents *prennent* beaucoup de photos. *D'en haut,* ils peuvent voir l'Arc de Triomphe, le Louvre, Sacré-Coeur, et la cathédrale de Notre Dame.

«Il faut visiter tous qu'on peut voir !» dit Katie.

«On a toute *une semaine,* on a temps de tout faire,» dit son père.

Quand il fait nuit, ils redescendent la tour et rentrent à l'hôtel.

«Qu'est-ce que vous voulez faire demain ?» demande la mère de Katie.

«Il va faire beau, dit Katie. On peut *commencer* à la cathédrale de Notre Dame. Après, on peut voir la Sainte Chapelle. *Les vitraux* sont très joli. La Sainte Chapelle est *à côté de* la Conciergerie. Ensuite, on peut traverser le fameux Pont Neuf pour aller voir le Louvre. Je sais qu'il y a des restaurants près du Louvre. On peut manger le déjeuner avant de visiter *le musée.*»

«On est à Paris toute la semaine, Katie ! dit Amy. On n'a pas besoin de tout voir demain.»

«Tu *as raison,* répond Katie. On peut visiter le Louvre le jour d'après.»

«Je veux voir Montmartre et la basilique de Sacré-Coeur,» dit la mère de Katie.

«Et moi, je veux voir le quartier du Marais et le Centre Pompidou, dit le père de Katie. J'aime bien l'art moderne.»

«On a besoin de visiter Versailles aussi ! ajoutent Katie et Amy. *Le palais* est très joli en été, mais il est *fermé* le lundi. Il faut faire attention.»

«Je *pense* qu'on a plein d'*idées*, dit le père de Katie. On commence demain avec la cathédrale de Notre Dame et l'Île de la Cité ?»

«Très bien !» disent les autres.

Ils *se couchent. Le lendemain* ils visitent la cathédrale de Notre Dame. Katie adore les *gargouilles.* Ils *goûtent* tous des crêpes avec du Nutella qui se vendent *devant* la cathédrale. A la Sainte Chapelle, ils *admirent* les vitraux jolis. A la Conciergerie, ils *apprennent* l'histoire de la Révolution Française. Quand ils rentrent à l'hôtel le soir, ils sont tous fatigués.

La semaine passe *vite.* Katie, sa mère, son père, et Amy visitent le Louvre et prennent des photos de la Joconde. Ils mangent des baguettes avec du *fromage* dans le Jardin des Tuileries et montent jusqu'au sommet de l'Arc de Triomphe. La mère de Katie achète une jolie *écharpe* à Montmartre et le père de Katie visite le Centre Pompidou. Pour visiter Versailles, ils prennent le RER. Le palais est *incroyable. Il y a* d'*or* partout. *Les jardins* sont très *beaux* aussi. Il y a beaucoup de *fleurs* et fontaines. Katie et Amy ne peuvent pas imaginer *vivre* dans *une maison* aussi cher.

Le jour du *départ* arrive. Katie ne veut pas partir. Elle a *beaucoup* appris à Paris. Elle reprends le RER jusqu'à l'aéroport avec sa mère, son père, et Amy. Quand l'avion *décolle*, elle regarde la ville par la fenêtre.

«Est-ce que tu as beaucoup aimé Paris, Katie ?» demande son père.

«Oui, je l'ai beaucoup aimé, répond Katie. J'ai finalement réalisé mon rêve de visiter Paris. Maintenant j'ai un *nouveau* rêve. Je veux revenir vivre en France un jour.»

A Trip

The airplane arrives at Roissy-Charles de Gaulle Airport around 10:00 A.M. Katie looks at the airport from the window of the airplane. She is in France!

Katies has dreamed for a long time of traveling to France. This year, she has finally had the chance to go abroad. She is visiting Paris with her mother, her father, and her best friend, Amy. Katie and Amy are sixteen years old and really like history. They want to learn the history of Paris on this trip.

Katie and her mother have found a fancy hotel downtown. To get to the hotel, they have to take the RER. Katie asks a gentleman how to buy tickets.

"Excuse me, sir. How do I buy tickets for the RER?"

"It's not difficult, young lady," replied the gentleman. "You can buy the tickets over there. You have to ask the lady behind the window."

"Thank you very much, sir," says Katie.

"I recommend that you buy tickets for the subway at the same time," says the gentleman. "It's easier. You can buy a book of ten tickets and it is less expensive."

"Thanks!" replies Katie. "I'll do that."

She buys from the lady four RER tickets and a book of subway tickets.

"How much does it cost?" asks Katie.

"It costs €54.50," replies the lady.

Katie thinks this is expensive, but she knows that vacation in Paris costs a lot. She gives the lady €60.

Katie, her mother, her father, and Amy get on the RER going towards Paris. The trip takes fifty minutes. Katie and Amy are very tired after the long trip in the airplane and they sleep a bit. Eventually, the small group arrives at the hotel. Katie shares a room with Amy and her parents share a second room.

"I need to take a nap," says Katie's father.

"Me too," says Amy.

All four decide to take a nap. After an hour, they go down to see the neighborhood.

"Oh! I can see the Eiffel Tower!" says Katie.

"Me too!" says Amy. "It's not far. Can we visit the Eiffel Tower this evening?"

"Why not?" say Katie's parents. "We are going to eat at a restaurant and afterward we can visit the Eiffel Tower."

They find a pretty little restaurant close to the hotel. The restaurant serves traditional French dishes. Katie and her father eat a delicious boeuf bourguignon. Her mother has a Niçoise salad. Amy is very adventurous and has snails. Katie's parents also drink a good French wine.

After dinner, they all walk towards the Eiffel Tower. Katie buys four tickets to go all the way up to the top of the tower. They decide to take the elevator because they don't want to climb 1,710 steps!

It was a good idea to visit the Eiffel Tower in the evening. When they get to the top, the sun is setting and the sky is orange, pink, and purple. Amy, Katie, and her parents take lots of photos. From so high up, they can see the Arc de Triomphe, the Louvre, Sacré-Coeur, and the cathedral of Notre Dame.

"We have to visit everything that we can see!" says Katie.

"We have a whole week, we have time to do everything," says her father.

When it gets dark, they go down from the tower and go back to the hotel.

"What would you all like to do tomorrow?" asks Katie's mother.

"It's going to be nice out," says Katie. "We can start with the cathedral of Notre Dame. Afterward, we can go see the Sainte Chapelle. The stained glass windows are very pretty. The Sainte Chapelle is next to the Conciergerie. Next, we can cross the famous Pont Neuf to go see the Louvre. I know there are restaurants close to the Louvre. We can eat lunch before visiting the museum."

"We're in Paris all week, Katie!" says Amy. "We don't have to see everything tomorrow."

"You're right," replies Katie. "We can visit the Louvre the day after."

"I'd like to see Montmartre and the Sacré-Coeur basilica," says Katie's mother.

"As for me, I'd like to see the Marais neighborhood and the Centre Pompidou," says Katie's father. "I really like modern art."

"We have to see Versailles too!" add Katie and Amy. "The palace is very pretty in the summer, but it's closed on Mondays. We have to be careful."

"I think we have plenty of ideas," says Katie's father. "Should we start tomorrow with the cathedral of Notre Dame?"

"Very good!" say the others.

They go to bed. The next day they visit the cathedral of Notre Dame. Katie loves the gargoyles. They try the crepes with Nutella that are sold in front of the cathedral. At the Sainte Chapelle, they admire the pretty stained glass windows. At the Conciergerie, they learn the history of the French Revolution. When they get back to the hotel in the evening, they are all tired.

The week goes quickly. Katie, her mother, her father, and Amy visit the Louvre and take pictures of the Mona Lisa. They eat baguettes with cheese in the Jardin des Tuileries and climb to the top of the Arc de Triomphe. Katie's mother buys a pretty scarf in Montmartre and Katie's father visits the Centre Pompidou. To visit Versailles, they take the RER. The palace is incredible. There is gold everywhere. The gardens are also very beautiful. There are many flowers and fountains. Katie and Amy can't imagine living in such an expensive house.

The day of their departure arrives. Katie doesn't want to leave. She has learned a lot in Paris. She takes the RER back to the airport with her mother, her father, and Amy. When the airplane takes off, she watches the city from the window.

"Did you like Paris a lot, Katie?" asks her father.

"Yes, I liked it a lot," replies Katie. "I finally fulfilled my dream of visiting Paris. Now I have a new dream. I want to come back and live in France someday."

Vocabulary, Grammar, and Comprehension Questions

<u>Nouns</u>

L'ascenseur (nm) = the elevator

L'avion (nm) = the airplane

Le carnet (de tickets) (nm) = the book of tickets, commonly sold for French public transportation

Le centre-ville (nm) = downtown

La chambre (nf) = the room, specifically the bedroom

Le départ (nm) = the departure

L'écharpe (nf) = the scarf

L'étranger (nm) = abroad

La fleur (nf) = the flower

La fontaine (nf) = the fountain

Le fromage (nm) = the cheese

La gargouille (nf) = the gargoyle

L'hôtel (nm) = the hotel, notice that the *l'* is used with words starting with *h*

L'idée (nf) = the idea

Le jardin (nm) = the garden, the yard

La maison (nf) = the house

Le musée (nm) = the museum

L'or (nm) = gold

Le palais (nm) = the palace

Le quartier (nm) = the neighborhood

La semaine (nf) = the week

La sieste (nf) = the nap

Le soir (nm) = the evening

Le sommet (nm) = the top, the summit

Le vin (nm) = the wine

Les vitraux (np) = the stained glass windows

Adjectives

Aventureux/euse(s) = adventurous

Beau(x)/Belle(s) = beautiful, handsome

Cher(s)/Chère(s) = expensive, a lot (in cost)

Facile(s) = easy

Fatigué(e)(s) = tired

Fermé(e)(s) = closed

Incroyable(s) = incredible

Joli(e)(s) = pretty

Meilleur(e)(s) = best, better

Nouveau(x)/elle(s) = new

Traditionnel(le)(s) = traditional

Adverbs

Beaucoup = a lot, very much

Loin = far, a long ways (away)

Longtemps = a long time

Vite = quickly, fast

Prepositions

A côté de = next to, beside

Après = after

Depuis = since

Devant = in front of

<u>Verbs</u>

Acheter = to buy

Admirer = to admire

Apprendre = to learn

Arriver = to arrive

Commencer = to start, to begin

Se coucher = to go to bed (reflexive verb)

Coûter = to cost

Decider = to decide

Décoller = to take off (in an airplane)

Dîner = to dine, to eat dinner/supper

Donner = to give

Goûter = to taste, to try (food)

Monter = to climb, to get into/on

Partager = to share

Partir = to leave

Penser = to think

Pouvoir = to be able to (can)

Prendre = to take

Regarder = to watch, to look at

Revenir = to come back

Rêver = to dream

Vivre = to live

<u>Useful Expressions</u>

Avoir besoin de = to need, conjugate *avoir* normally

Avoir raison = to be right/correct, conjugate *avoir* normally

Ça coûte combien ? = How much does it cost?

D'en haut = from above (point of view)

Excusez-moi = excuse me, formally

Il faut = it is necessary to, we should

Il y a = there are

Merci beaucoup = thank you very much

Pourquoi pas ? = Why not?

<u>Questions</u>

Répondez aux questions:

1. Katie visite Paris avec qui ?
2. Qu'est-ce que la mère de Katie achète à Montmartre ?
3. Combien coûtent les billets de RER et les tickets de métro que Katie achète ?
4. Le père de Katie veut visiter quel quartier ?
5. Quel est le nouveau rêve de Katie ?

Remplissez les blancs dans le texte. Il faut s'accorder les noms et les adjectifs.

1. Katie est _______________ (fatigué) après le voyage en avion.
2. Le palais de Versailles et la Tour Eiffel sont _______________ (incroyable).
3. Les musées en France sont _____________ (fermé) le lundi.
4. Ils ont une _____________ (beau) maison.

Remplissez les blancs dans le texte avec la préposition qui convient.

1. La Conciergerie est _______________ la Sainte Chapelle.
2. Ils ont visité la Tour Eiffel _____________ le dîner.
3. On peut acheter des crêpes _______________ la cathédrale de Notre Dame.

Conjuguez les verbes:

1. Pouvoir

Je	Nous
Tu	Vous
Il/Elle/On	Ils/Elles

2. Vivre

Je	Nous
Tu	Vous
Il/Elle/On	Ils/Elles

3. Apprendre

J'	Nous
Tu	Vous
Il/Elle/On	Ils/Elles

4. Partir

Je	Nous
Tu	Vous
Il/Elle/On	Ils/Elles

Answers in the back of book

*The Paris RER is a network of above- and below-ground commuter trains that link central Paris with the suburbs and towns that surround it. There are five lines: RER A, B, C, D, and E. Tourists are most likely to use RER A, which goes to Disneyland Paris, RER B, which goes to Roissy-Charles de Gaulle Airport, and RER C, which goes to Versailles. The RER also connects to the Paris Métro, or subway system, at a few of the stops. The Métro is a much denser system than the

RER and has three hundred stops within central Paris. There are fourteen lines in total and visitors to Paris are rarely more than a few minutes' walk from a station. To learn more about the transportation systems in Paris, the website www.parisbytrain.com is an excellent resource.

Chapter 4: A la Plage/At the Beach

A la Plage

Cyprien, Guillaume, et Clémence sont de bons amis. Aujourd'hui ils vont à *la plage*. Ils habitent dans le sud de la France et la plage n'est pas *loin*. Ils prennent la voiture.

Les trois amis préparent *un pique-nique avant* de partir.

«On a des *raisins* dans le frigo, dit Clémence. J'achète des sandwiches jambon-beurre* à *la boulangerie* à côté.»

«Je n'aime pas le sandwich jambon-beurre, répond Guillaume. Je veux un sandwich complet.»

«D'accord, j'achète un sandwich complet pour toi, Guillaume,» dit Clémence.

«Est-ce qu'on a des *biscuits* ?» demande Cyprien.

«Oui, on a des petits écoliers et des cookies*,» répond Clémence.

«Très bien, dit Cyprien. Moi, j'ai des *bouteilles* d'eau et des *bières.*»

«Et nous avons tous nos *maillots de bain* et nos *serviettes de bain* !» ajoute Clémence.

«Je pense qu'on a tous qu'il faut !» dit Guillaume.

Clémence achète trois sandwiches à la boulangerie et les trois amis montent dans la voiture. La voiture est petite et *vieille*, mais elle est *fiable*. Ils s'arrêtent *sur la route* pour acheter de *l'essence*. Clémence demande à Cyprien s'il a de *la crème solaire*.

«Non, répond Cyprien, je n'ai pas de crème solaire. Guillaume, est-ce que tu as de la crème solaire ?»

«Je n'ai pas de crème solaire *non plus*,» dit Guillaume.

«Ce n'est pas bien, dit Clémence. Je vais chercher de la crème solaire dans le magasin.»

Elle retourne dans cinq minutes avec une grande bouteille de crème solaire.

«Très bien ! dit Cyprien. Je ne veux pas de *coup de soleil*.»

Ils continuent de conduire. Après une demie-heure, ils arrivent à la plage. Il fait très beau. *Le ciel* et *la mer* sont bleus et il n'y a pas de *nuages*.

«On a bien fait de venir aujourd'hui ! dit Guillaume. Il n'y a pas trop de *monde*.»

Il a raison. Il n'y a pas beaucoup de personnes à la plage. Il y a de la place pour tout le monde. Cyprien, Guillaume, et Clémence trouvent *un endroit* joli pour mettre leurs serviettes de bain. Tous les trois *se changent*. Ils *mettent* leurs maillots de bain.

«Guillaume, est-ce que tu peux m'*aider* à mettre de la crème solaire ? demande Clémence. J'ai besoin de la crème solaire sur mon *dos*.»

«Bien sûr, Clémence,» répond Guillaume.

Quand ils sont tous bien protégés du soleil, ils *se baignent* dans la mer. L'eau est *chaude* et *les vagues* sont grandes. Les amis *nagent*, se parlent, et s'amusent bien dans l'eau. Après une heure, ils décident de manger leur pique-nique.

Clémence cherche les sandwiches, les raisins, les biscuits, et les bouteilles d'eau dans la voiture.

«Voilà, Guillaume, un sandwich complet pour toi, dit Clémence, et pour toi, Cyprien, un sandwich jambon-beurre.»

«N'oubliez pas de boire de l'eau, dit Guillaume. Il fait chaud.»

Les sandwiches et les raisins sont délicieux. Pour *le dessert*, ils mangent des biscuits.

«Je pense que je vais *me bronzer*, dit Clémence. Vous voulez que je cherche les bières dans la voiture avant ?»

«Non, je peux chercher les bières, dit Cyprien. Je vais boire de la bière et *lire un livre*.»

Il va à la voiture pour chercher les bières.

«Je vais me bronzer aussi,» dit Guillaume.

Cyprien lit son livre et Clémence et Guillaume se bronzent. *Le sable* est chaud et après quelques minutes Clémence et Guillaume *s'endorment*. Cyprien *rit*.

«Ils se bronzent, mais ils font aussi la sieste !» dit-il.

Une heure plus tard, Clémence et Guillaume se lèvent. Les trois amis décident de se baigner avant de partir. Ils nagent et jouent dans les vagues.

Guillaume regarde sa *montre*. Il est 16h.

«Il est 16h, Cyprien et Clémence, il dit. Je pense qu'il faut bientôt partir.»

«Tu as raison, Guillaume,» dit Cyprien.

Ils ramassent *les restes* du pique-nique, les serviettes de bain, les bières, et la bouteille de crème solaire. Ils montent dans la voiture.

«Il y a du sable *partout*, dit Clémence. Il y a du sable dans mes *cheveux*, dans mon maillot de bain, et dans mes *chaussures*.»

«Je sais, répond Cyprien. J'ai du sable dans mes cheveux aussi. Et je pense qu'il y avait du sable dans mon sandwich aujourd'hui.»

«Miam, un sandwich jambon-sable !» Guillaume rit.

«Est-ce qu'il y a encore des cookies ?» demande Clémence.

«Oui, ils sont ici,» répond Guillaume.

Il donne les cookies à Clémence. Elle partage les cookies avec Cyprien et Guillaume. Après une demi-heur, ils arrivent *chez* eux. Clémence rentre à l'appartement et se voit dans *un miroir*.

«Regardez ! dit Clémence. J'ai pris un coup de soleil !»

Ses *épaules* sont très *rouges*. Guillaume regarde.

«Oui, tu a pris un coup de soleil, il répond. Cyprien, est-ce que tu as pris un coup de soleil aussi ?»

«Non, dit Cyprien, ça va. J'ai mis de la crème solaire.»

«J'ai mis de la crème solaire aussi ! dit Clémence. Ce n'était pas *assez*. Ce n'est pas *grave*. Je vais prendre *une douche*. J'ai trop de sable dans mes cheveux.»

Guillaume met les serviettes de bain dans *la machine à laver*. Cyprien *jette* les restes du pique-nique à *la poubelle*. Ils décident de manger une salade pour le dîner et de regarder *une émission* de télévision avant de se coucher.

Le soir, Cyprien, Guillaume, et Clémence se couchent tôt. Ils sont tous fatigués après une longue journée à la plage. Ils sont très contents de vivre près de la plage et d'avoir de si bons amis.

At the Beach

Cyprien, Guillaume, and Clémence are good friends. Today, they are going to the beach. They live in the South of France, and the beach is not far away. They're taking the car.

The three friends prepare a picnic before leaving.

"We have grapes in the refrigerator," says Clémence. "I'm buying ham and butter sandwiches from the bakery next door."

"I don't like ham and butter sandwiches," replies Guillaume. "I want a sandwich with ham, cheese, lettuce, and eggs."

"Okay, I'll buy a sandwich with ham, cheese, lettuce, and eggs for you, Guillaume," says Clémence.

"Do we have cookies?" asks Cyprien.

"Yes, we have chocolate-covered shortbread and chocolate chip cookies," replies Clémence.

"Great," says Cyprien. "As for me, I have bottles of water and beer."

"And we all have our swimsuits and our beach towels!" adds Clémence.

"I think we have everything we need!" says Guillaume.

Clémence buys three sandwiches at the bakery, and the three friends get in the car. The car is small and old, but it is reliable. They stop on the way to buy gas. Clémence asks Cyprien if he has any sunscreen.

“No,” replies Cyprien, “I don’t have any sunscreen. Guillaume, do you have any sunscreen?”

“I don’t have any sunscreen either,” says Guillaume.

“That’s not good,” says Clémence. “I’m going to look for some sunscreen in the store.”

She comes back in five minutes with a big bottle of sunscreen.

“Excellent!” says Cyprien. “I don’t want a sunburn.”

They continue to drive. After a half hour, they arrive at the beach. It is very nice out. The sky and the sea are blue, and there are no clouds.

“We made a good decision to come today!” says Guillaume. “There aren’t too many people.”

He is right. There are not a lot of people on the beach. There is room for everyone. Cyprien, Guillaume, and Clémence find a pretty spot to put their beach towels. All three get changed. They put on their swimsuits.

“Guillaume, can you help me to put on some sunscreen?” asks Clémence. “I need sunscreen on my back.”

“Of course, Clémence,” replies Guillaume.

When they are all well protected from the sun, they go swimming in the sea. The water is warm and the waves are big. The friends swim, talk, and have a good time in the water. After an hour, they decide to eat their picnic.

Clémence gets the sandwiches, the grapes, the cookies, and the bottles of water from the car.

"Here you go, Guillaume, a sandwich with ham, cheese, lettuce, and eggs for you," says Clémence, "and for you, Cyprien, a ham and butter sandwich."

"Don't forget to drink water," says Guillaume. "It's hot out."

The sandwiches and the grapes are delicious. For dessert, they eat cookies.

"I'm going to tan," says Clémence. "Would you like me to get the beer from the car beforehand?"

"No, I can get the beer," says Cyprien. "I'm going to drink beer and read a book."

He goes to the car to get the beer.

"I'm going to tan as well," says Guillaume.

Cyprien reads his book and Clémence and Guillaume get tan. The sand is warm, and after a few minutes Clémence and Guillaume fall asleep. Cyprien laughs.

"They are getting tan, but they're also getting a nap!" he says.

An hour later, Clémence and Guillaume get up. The three friends decide to go swimming before leaving. They swim and play in the waves.

Guillaume looks at his watch. It is 4:00 P.M.

"It's 4:00, Cyprien et Clémence," he says. "I think we need to leave soon."

"You're right, Guillaume," says Cyprien.

They gather up the rest of the picnic, the beach towels, the beer, and the bottle of sunscreen. They get in the car.

"There is sand everywhere," says Clémence. "There is sand in my hair, in my swimsuit, and in my shoes."

"I know," replies Cyprien. "I have sand in my hair, too. And I think there was sand in my sandwich today."

"Yum, a ham–sand sandwich!" Guillaume laughs.

"Are there still some cookies?" asks Clémence.

"Yes, they're here," replies Guillaume.

He gives the cookies to Clémence. She shares the cookies with Cyprien and Guillaume. After a half hour, they arrive at their place. Clémence goes into the apartment and sees herself in a mirror.

"Look!" says Clémence. "I got a sunburn!"

Her shoulders are very red. Guillaume looks.

"Yes, you got a sunburn," he replies. "Cyprien, did you get a sunburn as well?"

"No," says Cyprien, "I'm okay. I put on sunscreen."

"I put on sunscreen too!" says Clémence. "It wasn't enough. It's not a big deal. I'm going to take a shower. I have too much sand in my hair."

Guillaume puts the beach towels in the washing machine. Cyprien throws the leftovers from the picnic in the garbage. They decide to have a salad for dinner and to watch a television show before going to bed.

In the evening, Cyprien, Guillaume, and Clémence go to bed early. They are all tired after a long day at the beach. They are very happy to live close to the beach and to have such good friends.

Vocabulary, Grammar, and Comprehension Questions

<u>Nouns</u>

La bière (nf) = the beer

Le biscuit (nm) = the cookie

La boulangerie (nf) = the bakery

La bouteille (nf) = the bottle

Le ciel (nm) = the sky, the heavens

La chaussure (nf) = the shoe

Les cheveux (np) = the hair

Le coup de soleil (nm) = the sunburn

La crème solaire (nf) = the sunscreen

Le dessert (nm) = the dessert

Le dos (nm) = the back (body part)

La douche (nf) = the shower

L'émission (nf) = the (television) show

L'endroit (nm) = the place

L'épaule (nf) = the shoulder

L'essence (nf) = the gasoline

Le livre (nm) = the book

La machine à laver (nf) = the washing machine

Le maillot de bain (nm) = the swimsuit

La mer (nf) = the sea, the ocean

Le miroir (nm) = the mirror

La montre (nf) = the wristwatch

Le nuage (nm) = the cloud

La plage (nf) = the beach

Le pique-nique (nm) = the picnic

La poubelle (nf) = the garbage (can)

Le raisin (nm) = the grape

Les restes (np) = the leftovers

Le sable (nm) = the sand

La serviette de bain (nf) = the towel, the beach towel

La vague (nf) = the wave

Adjectives

Chaud(e)(s) = warm, hot

Fiable(s) = trustworthy, dependable

Grave(s) = serious

Rouge(s) = red, reddened

Vieux/Vieille(s) = old

Adverbs

Assez = enough

Avant = before

Loin = far, a long way

Partout = everywhere

Verbs

Aider = to help

Se baigner = to go swimming, to bathe (reflexive verb)

Se bronzer = to tan, to go tanning (reflexive verb)

Se changer = to change clothes (reflexive verb)

S'endormir = to go to sleep (reflexive verb)

Jeter = to throw, to toss

Lire = to read

Mettre = to put (on)

Nager = to swim

Rire = to laugh

<u>Useful Expressions</u>

Sur la route = on the road, on the way

Non plus = either, neither. Used in negative sentences.

Monde = literally means "world," but also refers to "people in general," as in the expression "tout le monde"

Chez = a preposition that means "at a person's home," so "chez Julie" means "at Julie's house." Also used to refer to businesses: "chez le médecin" = "at the doctor's."

<u>Questions</u>

Répondez aux questions:

1. Où habitent Clémence, Guillaume, et Cyprien ?
2. Guillaume préfère quel sandwich ?
3. Qu'est-ce que les trois amis oublient ?
4. Clémence et Guillaume se bronzent. Qu'est-ce que Cyprien fait ?
5. Est-ce que Clémence a mis assez de crème solaire ? Pourquoi ?

Remplissez les blancs avec l'adverbe qui convient:

assez	avant	loin	partout

1. J'ai mangé _____________ de venir.
2. Je trouve du sable _____________.
3. Mes parent habitent _____________ de moi.
4. Est-ce que tu as bu _____________ d'eau ?

Conjuguez les verbes:

1. Nager

Je	Nous
Tu	Vous
Il/Elle/On	Ils/Elles

2. Jeter

Je	Nous
Tu	Vous
Il/Elle/On	Ils/Elles

3. Lire

Je	Nous
Tu	Vous
Il/Elle/On	Ils/Elles

4. Mettre

Je	Nous
Tu	Vous

Il/Elle/On	Ils/Elles

Answers in the back of book

*French bakeries sell fresh breads and often a variety of pastries, but they also sell ready-made, wrapped sandwiches that are a quick and easy meal option. The most famous of these sandwiches is the *jambon–beurre*, or ham–butter sandwich. The sandwich is exactly how it sounds: plenty of salted butter with cold deli ham on a baguette. Other, fancier sandwiches include cheese, salad, tomatoes, and sliced hard-boiled eggs. The *complet* sandwich that Guillaume wants has all of these toppings. It's also common to find tuna salad sandwiches, and some bakeries have their own specialties. The *jambon-beurre*, however, remains a French favorite.

*When the French don't buy desserts at the bakery or pastry shop, they often get packaged cookies. There are many types of these cookies in France. One popular cookie company is the brand *LU*, and their products can occasionally be found in American grocery stores. The *petit écolier* cookie in this story is a rectangular shortbread cookie with a chocolate topping. The name of the cookie refers to the image of a little schoolboy that is molded in the chocolate. Chocolate chip cookies are not a traditional French food, but they are getting more and more popular. In French, the English word *cookie* has become the word for any cookie with pieces of chocolate or M&M candy mixed in.

Chapter 5: Mon Anniversaire/My Birthday

Mon Anniversaire

Aujourd'hui, c'est le jour de mon anniversaire. J'ai vingt-cinq ans et j'ai *invité* tous mes amis de *fêter* ce grand jour avec moi ce soir.

J'ai *du* acheter beaucoup de *choses à manger* pour ma fête d'anniversaire. Il y a trois jours, je suis allé au *supermarché*. J'avais besoin des *gâteaux secs* et des *boissons* pour *l'apéritif.** Pour le dîner, je fais des *pâtes* avec de *la sauce tomate*, une *salade*, et une *assiette* de fromages. On va manger un délicieux gâteau d'anniversaire pour le dessert.

Au supermarché, j'ai acheté des spaghettis. J'aime bien le spaghetti. J'ai acheté de *la viande hachée*, des tomates, des *épices*, et des *champignons* pour la sauce tomate. Je préfère la sauce tomate *fait-maison*. J'ai pris une salade aux *épinards* et quelques fromages différents. J'aime le camembert et le chèvre, mais mes amis préfère le brie et le roquefort. Les pâtes, la sauce tomate, la salade, et les fromages ne sont pas très compliqués à préparer. Le gâteau, *par contre*, est un peu difficile.

J'ai acheté de *la farine*, du *sucre*, du *sel*, des *oeufs*, de *la levure chimique*, et du chocolat pour faire le gâteau. J'ai aussi acheté des fruits frais pour *décorer* le gâteau. J'aime les fruits rouges: les *fraises*, les *framboises*, les *cerises*, et les *groseilles*. Le gâteau au chocolat va être très joli avec les fruits rouges.

J'ai *presque oublié* les boissons ! On *boit toujours* beaucoup quand on fête mon anniversaire. J'ai pris du *jus d'orange*, du vin blanc, et du *cassis* pour l'apéritif. Je *mélange* le vin blanc et le cassis pour fair *un kir*. C'est très bon. Pour le dîner, j'ai acheté un vin rouge de Bordeaux. Les vins de Bordeaux sont très *connu*. J'ai pris également du *cidre* Breton. J'ai une amie qui ne boit que du cidre. Finalement, j'ai acheté des bières. On ne peut pas *faire la fête* sans des bières !*

Ce matin, je me suis levé tôt pour tout préparer. J'ai commencé avec le gâteau. J'ai mélangé la farine, le sucre, le sel, et la levure chimique. Ensuite, j'ai *ajouté* des oeufs et du chocolat *fondu*. J'ai mis le gâteau au *four* pendant quarante-cinq minutes. Le gâteau *a l'air* trop bon !

J'ai fait la sauce tomate après le gâteau. J'ai *coupé* les tomates et les champignons en petits *morceaux* et j'ai fait *dorer* la viande dans une grande *casserole* avec de *l'huile d'olive*. Puis j'ai ajouté les tomates et les champignons. Finalement, j'ai ajouté de *l'eau* et des épices. J'ai *laissé cuire* la sauce pendant trente minutes.

Vers 19h* j'ai préparé la salade dans un grand *bol*. J'ai coupé les fruits rouges et j'ai fait une décoration jolie sur le gâteau au chocolat. J'ai mis les gâteaux secs dans quelques petits bols et j'ai trouvé des *verres* pour l'apéritif. J'ai mis le vin blanc dans *le frigo*.

Maintenant il est 20h. Mes amis vont *bientôt* arriver et on va prendre l'apéritif. A 20h30 je vais cuire les pâtes et on va manger le dîner vers 20h45. Après, on va manger du fromage. C'est normal en France de manger du fromage après le dîner. *De temps en temps*, on mange du fromage comme dessert. Mais ce soir on a du gâteau aussi. Je sais que mes amis vont me chanter la chanson «Joyeux Anniversaire.» Ensuite, on va *chercher* les bières et on va faire la fête ! L'année *dernière*, mes amis sont rentrés à la maison vers 3h du matin. Je sais qu'on va bien *s'amuser* cette année aussi.

J'entends quelqu'un *frapper* à *la porte* ! C'est un de mes amis. J'*arrête* d'*écrire*. Maintenant il faut fêter mon anniversaire !

My Birthday

Today is my birthday. I'm twenty-five years old, and I've invited all my friends to celebrate this big day with me tonight.

I had to buy lots of things to eat for my birthday party. Three days ago, I went to the grocery store. I needed crackers and drinks for the pre-dinner drinks. For dinner, I'm making pasta with tomato sauce, a salad, and a cheese plate. We're going to eat a delicious birthday cake for dessert.

At the grocery store, I bought spaghetti. I like spaghetti a lot. I bought ground meat, tomatoes, spices, and mushrooms for the tomato sauce. I prefer homemade tomato sauce. I chose a spinach salad and a few different cheeses. I like camembert and goat cheese, but my friends prefer brie and blue cheese. The pasta, the tomato sauce, the salad, and the cheeses aren't too complicated to prepare. The cake, on the other hand, is a little difficult.

I bought flour, sugar, salt, eggs, baking powder, and chocolate to make the cake. I also bought some fresh fruit to decorate the cake. I like red fruits: strawberries, raspberries, cherries, and currants. The chocolate cake will be very pretty with the red fruits.

I almost forgot drinks! We always drink a lot when we celebrate my birthday. I got orange juice, white wine, and blackcurrant liqueur for the pre-dinner drinks. I mix the white wine with the blackcurrant liqueur to make *kir*. It's very good. For dinner, I bought a red wine from Bordeaux. The wines from Bordeaux are very well-known. I also got Breton cider. I have a friend who only drinks cider. Finally, I bought beer. It's not possible to have a party without beer!

This morning, I got up early in order to prepare everything. I started with the cake. I mixed the flour, sugar, salt, and baking powder. Next, I added eggs and melted chocolate. I put the cake in the oven for forty-five minutes. The cake looks really good!

I made the tomato sauce after the cake. I cut the tomatoes and mushrooms in little pieces, and I browned the meat in a big pot with olive oil. Then I added the tomatoes and the onions. Finally, I added water and spices. I let the sauce cook for thirty minutes.

Around 7:00 P.M. I prepared the salad in a big bowl. I cut the red fruits and I made a pretty decoration on the chocolate cake. I put the crackers in several small bowls, and I found glasses for the pre-dinner drinks. I put the white wine in the refrigerator.

Now it is 8:00 P.M. My friends will arrive soon and we'll have pre-dinner drinks. At 8:30 P.M. I will cook the pasta and we will eat dinner around 8:45 P.M. Afterwards, we will eat cheese. It's normal in France to eat cheese after dinner. Sometimes, we eat cheese as dessert. But this evening we have cake as well. I know that my friends will sing the song "Happy Birthday." Next, we'll find the beer and have a party! Last year, my friends went home around 3:00 A.M. I know that we'll have a good time this year too.

I hear someone knocking at the door! It's one of my friends. I'll stop writing. Now I have to celebrate my birthday!

Vocabulary, Grammar, and Comprehension Questions

<u>Nouns</u>

L'apéritif (nm) = the pre-dinner drinks, the aperitif

L'assiette (nf) = the plate

La boisson (nf) = the drink

Le bol (nm) = the bowl

La casserole (nf) = the casserole dish/saucepan

Le cassis (nm) = the blackcurrant liqueur

La cerise (nf) = the cherry

Le champignon (nm) = the mushroom

Le cidre (nm) = the cider

Les épices (np) = the spices

Les épinards (np) = the spinach

La farine (nf) = the flour

Le four (nm) = the oven

La fraise (nf) = the strawberry

La framboise (nf) = the raspberry

Le gâteau sec (nm) = the cracker

La groseille (nf) = the red currant

L'huile d'olive (nf) = the olive oil

Le jus d'orange (nm) = the orange juice

Le kir (nm) = alcoholic drink made of white wine and blackcurrant liqueur

La levure chimique (nf) = the baking powder

Le morceau (nm) = the piece, the bit (of something)

L'oeuf (nm) = the egg

Les pâtes (np) = the pasta

La salade (nf) = the salad

La sauce tomate (nf) = the tomato sauce

Le sel (nm) = the salt

Le sucre (nm) = the sugar

Le supermarché (nm) = the grocery store

Le verre (nm) = the drinking glass

La viande (nf) = the meat

Adjectives

Connu(e)(s) = known, well-known

Dernier(s)/ère(s) = last, previous

Fondu(e)(s) = melted

Haché(e)(s) = minced or ground, referring to meat

Adverbs

Bientôt = soon

Presque = almost

Toujours = always

Verbs

Ajouter = to add

S'amuser = to amuse oneself (reflexive verb)

Arrêter = to stop

Boire = to drink

Chercher = to search (for)

Connaître = to know (a person), to be familiar with

Couper = to cut

Cuire = to cook

Dorer = to brown, as in meat or vegetables

Ecrire = to write

Fêter = to celebrate

Frapper = to knock, to hit

Inviter = to invite

Laisser = to let/permit, to leave (be)

Mélanger = to mix

Oublier = to forget

Useful Expressions

Avoir l'air (de) = to look (like), to seem

De temps en temps = from time to time, sometimes

Faire la fête = to party, to go out, often implies alcohol consumption

Fait-maison = homemade

Par contre = on the other hand

Quelque chose à manger = something to eat

Questions

Répondez aux questions:

1. Qu'est-ce que je prépare pour mon dîner d'anniversaire ?
2. Comment est-ce qu'on fait le *kir* ?
3. A quelle heure est-ce qu'ils vont manger ?
4. Qu'est-ce qu'ils prennent comme dessert ?

Conjuguez le verbe en utilisant le passé composé. N'oubliez pas *avoir* ou *être*.

1. Je ______________ (arriver) à 20h.
2. Il ______________ (décorer) le gâteau avec des fruits.
3. Ses amis ________________ (frapper) à la porte.
4. Nous ________________ (chercher) des framboises.
5. Est-ce que tu ________________ (oublier) la bière ?
6. L'année dernière, j'______________ (fêter) mon anniversaire.
7. Elizabeth ______________ (inviter) ses parents à la fête.
8. Est-ce que vous ________________ (mélanger) les tomates et les champignons ?
9. Elles ______________ (boire) du cidre.
10. Il ______________ (écrire) un article dans un journal.

Answers in the back of book

*The partygoers in this story are having an *apéritif* before dinner. While aperitifs, or pre-dinner drinks, certainly exist in the United States, they are much more common in France. Americans might call this tradition a *cocktail hour*, and those usually only take place before fancy events like wedding receptions or gala dinners. In France, it is common for hosts to organize an *apéritif*, or *apéro*, whenever they have someone over in the afternoon, even if their guests will not be staying for dinner. The *apéro* does not have to include alcoholic drinks, although it often does. Juice, wine, mixed drinks like the *kir*, and stronger alcohol like whiskey are common. Drinks are usually accompanied by small snacks, which can be as simple as bowls of crackers. French grocery stores sell lots of crackers and cookies for the *apéro*. There also might be sliced sausages or cheeses.

*The drinking age in France is eighteen, but until 2010 it was sixteen, and in practice the French are fairly lax about checking for identification and generally allow younger teens to drink alcohol in the company of their parents. At twenty-five, the narrator of this story would not have any trouble buying alcohol. The French have a reputation for having a smart, moderate approach to alcohol, but the change in the drinking age was actually brought about by evidence of increased binge drinking among young people. France is of course known for its wine, which is produced all over the country but especially in the south. Brittany and Normandy are known for hard cider, and there is a wide variety of regionally-produced liqueurs throughout France. Beer is made in France, but some of the most popular and inexpensive beers are Belgian. The French often drink beer at room temperature.

*The French use the twenty-four-hour clock, also known as military time, and indicate times in writing by adding an *h* to the number. The *h* stands for *heures*, so "Il est 15h30" would be said "Il est quinze heures trente." It's common to write *0h* for midnight and *12h* for noon, but those times are usually said as "minuit" and "midi," respectively, rather than "zero heures" and "douze heures."

Conclusion

Félicitations d'avoir fini ce livre !

Congratulations on reaching the end of this book! French is a challenging language to master, and by working on your reading, you are sure to have come a long way. I hope that you have learned a lot of new vocabulary, practiced your grammar, and become more comfortable with French syntax. Now that you have finished this book, don't stop reading French! Don't be discouraged by more difficult texts. With time and patience, your French reading skills will improve.

I hope you have enjoyed this book in the *Learn French* series. I have tried to write the book I wish I had read when I was first learning French. If you enjoyed the book and found it helpful, a review on Amazon is always appreciated!

Answers

Chapter 1

Répondez aux questions:

1. Les soeurs de Manon s'appellent Camille et Eugénie.
2. Manon visite ses grands-parents le dimanche.
3. Simon a treize ans.
4. Eugénie étudie l'anglais à l'université.
5. Manon a une nièce.

Remplissez les blancs dans le texte avec le mot qui convient:

Manon habite avec ses <u>parents</u> et son <u>frère</u>. Ses deux <u>soeurs</u> étudient à l'<u>université</u>. Son frère Vincent est <u>marié</u>. Sa femme <u>s'appelle</u> Agnès. Ils ont deux <u>enfants</u>. Manon aime sa grande <u>famille</u>.

Conjuguez les verbes:

1. Avoir

J'ai	Nous avons
Tu as	Vous avez
Il/Elle/On a	Ils/Elles ont

2. Être

Je suis	Nous sommes
Tu es	Vous êtes
Il/Elle/On est	Ils/Elles sont

3. Aller

Je vais	Nous allons
Tu vas	Vous allez
Il/Elle/On va	Ils/Elles vont

4. Vouloir

Je veux	Nous voulons
Tu veux	Vous voulez
Il/Elle/On veut	Ils/Elles veulent

Chapter 2

Répondez aux questions:

1. Axelle porte sa robe préférée.
2. Axelle dessine sa famille: sa mère, son père, et elle.
3. C'est un grand jour parce qu'Axelle peut choisir un chaton.
4. Le nom du chaton est Loulou.

Remplissez les blancs dans le texte:

1. Axelle est une <u>petite</u> fille.
2. Axelle et son père sont <u>blonds</u>.
3. Aujourd'hui, le métro est <u>comblé</u>.
4. Les institutrices sont <u>grandes</u>.

Conjuguez les verbes:

1. Faire

Je fais	Nous faisons
Tu fais	Vous faites

Il/Elle/On fait	Ils/Elles font

2. Jouer

Je joue	Nous jouons
Tu joues	Vous jouez
Il/Elle/On joue	Ils/Elles jouent

3. Savoir

Je sais	Nous savons
Tu sais	Vous savez
Il/Elle/On sait	Ils/Elles savent

4. Voir

Je vois	Nous voyons
Tu vois	Vous voyez
Il/Elle/On voit	Ils/Elles voient

Chapter 3

Répondez aux questions:

1. Katie visite Paris avec sa mère, son père, et sa meilleure amie Amy.
2. La mère de Katie achète une écharpe à Montmartre.
3. Les billets de RER et les tickets de métro coûtent €54.50.
4. Le père de Katie veut visiter le quartier du Marais.
5. Le nouveau rêve de Katie est de revenir vivre en France.

Remplissez les blancs dans le texte:

1. Katie est <u>fatiguée</u> après le voyage en avion.

2. Le palais de Versailles et la Tour Eiffel sont <u>incroyables</u>.
3. Les musées en France sont <u>fermés</u> le lundi.
4. Ils ont une <u>belle</u> maison.

Remplissez les blancs dans le texte avec la préposition qui convient.

1. La Conciergerie est <u>à côté de</u> la Sainte Chapelle.
2. Ils ont visité la Tour Eiffel <u>après</u> le dîner.
3. On peut acheter des crêpes <u>devant</u> la cathédral de Notre Dame.

Conjuguez les verbes:

1. Pouvoir

Je peux	Nous pouvons
Tu peux	Vous pouvez
Il/Elle/On peut	Ils/Elles peuvent

2. Vivre

Je vis	Nous vivons
Tu vis	Vous vivez
Il/Elle/On vit	Ils/Elles vivent

3. Apprendre

J'apprends	Nous apprenons
Tu apprends	Vous apprenez
Il/Elle/On apprend	Ils/Elles apprennent

4. Partir

Je pars	Nous partons

| Tu pars | Vous partez |
| Il/Elle/On part | Ils/Elles partent |

Chapter 4

Répondez aux questions:

1. Clémence, Guillaume, et Cyprien habitent dans le sud de la France.
2. Guillaume préfère un sandwich complet.
3. Les trois amis oublient la crème solaire.
4. Cyprien lit un livre et boit des bières.
5. Clémence n'a pas mis assez de crème solaire. Elle a pris un coup de soleil.

Remplissez les blancs avec l'adverbe qui convient:

1. J'ai mangé <u>avant</u> de venir.
2. Je trouve du sable <u>partout</u>.
3. Mes parents habitent <u>loin</u> de moi.
4. Est-ce que tu as bu <u>assez</u> d'eau ?

Conjuguez les verbes:

1. Nager

Je nage	Nous nageons
Tu nages	Vous nagez
Il/Elle/On nage	Ils/Elles nagent

2. Jeter

| Je jette | Nous jetons |
| Tu jettes | Vous jetez |

| Il/Elle/On jette | Ils/Elles jettent |

3. Lire

Je lis	Nous lisons
Tu lis	Vous lisez
Il/Elle/On lit	Ils/Elles lisent

4. Mettre

Je mets	Nous mettons
Tu mets	Vous mettez
Il/Elle/On met	Ils/Elles mettent

Chapter 5

Répondez aux questions:

1. Je prépare des spaghettis, une sauce tomate, une salade, du fromage, et un gâteau pour mon dîner d'anniversaire.
2. On fait le *kir* avec du vin blanc et du cassis.
3. Ils vont manger à 20h45.
4. Ils prennent un gâteau au chocolat comme dessert.

Conjuguez le verbe en utilisant le passé composé. N'oubliez pas *avoir* ou *être*.

1. Je <u>suis arrivé(e)</u> à 20h.
2. Il <u>a décoré</u> le gâteau avec des fruits.
3. Ses amis <u>ont frappé</u> à la porte.
4. Nous <u>avons cherché</u> des framboises.
5. Est-ce que tu <u>as oublié</u> la bière ?
6. L'année dernière, j'<u>ai fêté</u> mon anniversaire.
7. Elizabeth <u>a invité</u> ses parents à la fête.
8. Est-ce que vous <u>avez mélangé</u> les tomates et les champignons?

9. Elles <u>ont bu</u> du cidre.
10. Il <u>a écrit</u> un article dans un journal.

Help me improve this book

While I have never met you, if you made it through this book I know that you are the kind of person that is wanting to get better and is willing to take on tough feedback to get to that point. You and I are cut from the same cloth in that respect. I am always looking to get better and I wish to not just improve myself, but also this book. If you have positive feedback, please take the time to leave a review. It will help other find this book and it can help change a life in the same way that it changed yours. If you have constructive feedback, please also leave a review. It will help me better understand what you, the reader, need to make significant improvements in your life. I will take your feedback and use it to improve this book so that it can become more powerful and beneficial to all those who encounter it.

REMEMBER TO JOIN THE GROUP NOW!

 If you have not joined the Mastermind Self Development group yet, now is your time! You will receive videos and articles from top authorities in self development as well as a special group only offers on new books and training programs. There will also be a monthly member only draw that gives you a chance to win any book from your Kindle wish list!

If you sign up through this link http://www.mastermindselfdevelopment.com/specialreport you will also get a special free report on the Wheel of Life. This report will give you a visual look at your current life and then take you through a series of exercises that will help you plan what your perfect life looks like. The workbook does not end there; we then take you through a process to help you plan how to achieve that perfect life. The process is very powerful and has the potential to change your life forever. Join the group now and start to change your life!
http://www.mastermindselfdevelopment.com/specialreport

You will also love these other great titles from Mastermind Self Development!

You will want to check out these other great titles Mastermind Self Development. All available in the Kindle store or you can just click on covers below.

myBook.to/positivelove

http://mybook.to/minimalism30days

You can also find these titles by searching them in the Kindle store on Amazon.

Learning Languages:

A Fast and easy guide for beginners to learn any foreign language

Free membership into the Mastermind Self Development Group!

For a limited time, you can join the Mastermind Self Development Group for free! You will receive videos and articles from top authorities in self development as well as a special group only offers on new books and training programs. There will also be a monthly member only draw that gives you a chance to win any book from your Kindle wish list!

If you sign up through this link http://www.mastermindselfdevelopment.com/specialreport specialreport you will also get a special free report on the Wheel of Life. This report will give you a visual look at your current life and then take you through a series of exercises that will help you plan what your perfect life looks like. The workbook does not end there; we then take you through a process to help you plan how to achieve that perfect life. The process is very powerful and has the potential to change your life forever. Join the group now and start to change your life! http://www.mastermindselfdevelopment.com/specialreport

Table of Contents

Introduction

Congratulations on downloading Learning Languages: A Fast and easy guide for beginners to learn any foreign language and thank you for doing so.

The following chapters will discuss the best way for you to learn a brand new language - any language that you'd like to, in fact.

This whole book is based off of a technique that I've developed in quite a while of studying language. I've found that it's the method which works best with my brain in particular. The method is based around breaking down language learning into small easy to learn chunks, *understanding* the core concepts underlying each and every language that you work with, as well as emphasizing the concept of immersion.

I have a huge number of qualms with conventional language learning techniques. For a long time, the typical manner used to learn another language was to simply start from the very beginning.

Language learning is like learning anything else, and frankly, if you're trying to teach a child mathematics, you don't teach them subtraction one week and then long division the very next, because long division builds off of other concepts that you've already worked with before.

However, as a result of the information age, the language learning paradigm has dramatically shifted. It started with somewhat of a shift back in the 1990s when early forms of language learning software began to hit the market. And, certainly, one could always go to the local bookstore and pick up this or that book, and even get engrossed in various methods such as the *Pimsleur* method. If they wanted to be immersed, their options were either moving to the country of the language they wanted to learn, special ordering books (and VHS tapes after a while), or watching Spanish television if they were learning Spanish in particular.

In other words, linguistics became a rather exclusive club. Today, you can just Google "how to speak Korean" or "how to speak Danish" and go from there. Even 20 years ago, though, that was hardly an option.

So in the last 20 years, we've made astronomical strides in terms of language learning. Immersion focused learning has generally been regarded, hands down, as the best and most effective way to learn a language. There are manifold reasons to this, but the biggest is that we are born to learn language.

Think about it like this: the Earth is absolutely *full* of creatures. Different species roam everywhere. The world is littered with different animals which took different evolutionary paths and yet humans are the only ones with language. Why is this?

Well, because if we didn't have it, then frankly we'd be at the bottom of the food chain. We diverged in such a way that we had to figure out how to work together towards common goals. We had to learn how to work together and communicate. So in a sense, your brain is not only *driven* to learn more languages. It's in fact explicitly *motivated* to learn language, whether it be early on in our lives or at a later point. We are *made* to learn and speak language. Saying anything else is terribly dishonest to ourselves.

The fastest way for us to learn languages is to immerse in it as much as possible, because such a method taps into those historic and prehistoric methods of language acquisition that we had to adapt to and still have to adapt today, if not even *more* so due to the fact that society has gotten so advanced to the point that we literally cannot live without learning another language.

Because immersion is such a great way to learn a language, language-learning methods which are *centered* around immersion have actually started popping up since the advent of the information age. An example of such is the extremely popular Benny Lewis's Fluent in 3 Months program; this Irish linguistic anomaly went from a person who only spoke English to somebody who now speaks seven languages fluently and four well. There are also numerous websites and applications which aim to teach one specifically how to use various languages, or vocabulary at the very least. As you very well may have guessed, we're going to be trying to implementing those into our language learning process to some extent in a manner which we'll discuss more later.

So what exactly is this book's approach? Well, you may have bought it alongside my others, or you may have bought it as a stand-alone book. Its first purpose is to accompany my other books I've written as a means of offering you a surefire way to become an absolutely fantastic speaker of any language. However, its secondary purpose is to outline a cohesive method of language learning that will really help you to get to the bulk of the language that you wish to learn and ascend to linguistic heights that you're only daydreaming of right now.

So in that pursuit, here are the things which this book is going to attempt to do.

First, you need to get into the mindset of language learning. So many people talk about how they can't do this or that. The rest of the book will be rather technical, but learning a language - as with learning anything else - requires a lot of dedication and, indeed, confidence in your ability to perform with it.

The second thing that we're going to talk about is analyzing the key concepts of a language, recognizing its differences from your own rather than its similarities, and then indeed learning and applying the essential concepts of the language.. If you've read or will read any of my other books, you'll notice that this is indeed a rather common motif that I express regularly. In my opinion, there is nothing more necessary and paramount when you're learning a new language than having a firm grasp on the grammatical concepts underlying said language. I'll discuss in greater detail why this is absolutely necessary in chapter two.

The third thing that we're going to cover is the absolutely critical importance of immersion and how to use it to your benefit in order to build your knowledge of the language as well as your vocabulary. I heavily disagree with the academic method of teaching vocabulary to wishful language students by heaping it on them and making them memorize it for an upcoming test and then hardly using it again if it's not related to the next pertinently covered topic. But that's a grievance for another day (or another chapter, at least.)

The fourth and final thing that we're going to cover and which makes up this method in an essential manner is the importance of *usage*. Usage is the point at which a lot of the previously talked about topics come together and usage is what is actually going to teach you to speak and communicate in the language. *Usage* in some contexts will also naturally build your vocabulary as well as reinforcing some bizarre concepts which may otherwise escape you, like the conjugation of irregular verbs.

So that makes up the four points of my language learning methodology: *study* the history, *break down* the language, *immerse* yourself, and *use* what you've learned. It's very bare-bones and my presentations of these given topics haven't been as great due to the brevity with which I'm presenting them, but you've got my solemn guarantee that everything will click for you as you read this book just as it did for me.

There are plenty of books on this subject on the market, thanks again for choosing this one! Every effort was made to ensure it is full of as much useful information as possible, please enjoy!

Chapter 1: Get into the Mindset

There are two different primary mindsets to language acquisition in the world right now. There are more in other subsets, but the two most commonly encountered are the academic sort - the sort which has you sitting in a classroom, possibly all day, drilling you with vocabulary lessons and grammatical concepts in an academic context - and the immersive sort - these are the ones which are generally espoused by polyglots, so I think that taking time in order to establish how you can work within this framework is super important.

I don't think there's anything explicitly wrong with the academic manner. But I do think it has its shortcomings as a form of language pedagogy intended for simple and natural language learning.

The reason that we use classrooms in order to teach things and we teach in such book-based ways in general is that teaching the myriad lessons which are taught at an institution like so demands that one have dedicated linear study. For a great many things, this works well. Mathematics, a musical instrument, chemistry, and so forth. For linguistics, it *can* work, but it's very far detached from our natural forms of language learning.

What actually works best for linguistics, many have found - it's not a universal thing, remember, but it's just the thing which works best for the majority of people - is an *immersion* based learning experience. Or in other words, an experience where they're surrounded by the language and are practicing it not just in the context of tests and flash cards, but in the television they watch, the applications on their phone, the people that they talk to, and so on.

I've spoken to a lot of people in my life who have tried to learn this or that language. They always tell me that "I'm just not cut out for learning languages" or something like that, and it's absurd.

I'm going to be honest: the traditional methods for language learning require a certain amount of passivity. We aren't made to learn language passively. It's not something that we're created to do. And when people are sitting in classrooms learning drab vocab which may or may not be something they'll actually talk about, I can't help feel like there's a lack of proper action or motivation. Often, too, that's what will kill the person's ability to learn: an utter lack of motivation due to the fact that they couldn't care less about the thing they're learning.

Let me make this clear: language learning is *not* easy. It can be made *easier*, but it's not *easy*. Saying that you expect to learn a language in a month or with only ten minutes of practice a day is a lot like those diet pills that proclaim themselves to be some kind of snake oil that will make you shed 100 pounds in a year: it doesn't happen. Full stop. It is *possible* to learn a language very quickly - in two to three months - with absolute dedication and what actually totals out to a lot of hard work, just like it's *possible* to lose 100 pounds in a year. However, it is not a passive activity.

Language learning happens in three ways:

1) Receiving input
2) Generating output
3) Receiving feedback/correction

It's through these three alone that you're going to learn a language. The input could be anything. It could be a gigantic "For Dummies" book that walks through every step of the language for beginners, or it could be a barebones explanatory sheet that teachers the person the basics before putting them on their own.

The output happens in one way only: you personally creating the phrases from the concepts that you know and from the things that you know. This is the only way that output can happen.

Receiving feedback and correction happens through somebody more proficient in the language than you are correcting you on this topic or that of the language after hearing you speak. They could be anybody from a teacher to a pen-pal to a girlfriend who was fluent in the language. It doesn't matter, what matters is that somehow and some way you're getting it.

So with those aspects of language learning fleshed out, now what we need to settle is how we can get those. The fact is that a lot of people, and in fact a lot of traditional language learning systems, will put up a fight against these natural language learning mechanisms. But I refuse to do that.

Here are the things that I'm going to emphasize from a standpoint of your demeanor towards language learning:

- *Passion* for the language
- *Connection* to the content
- *Immersion* rather than arbitrary rote memorization
- *Confidence* in your ability to speak
- *Willingness* to go out of your comfort zone.

You need a *passion* for the language if you want to learn it. Even a fake one, if you have to conjure one up out of thin air. At the beginning, learning a language is going to be awful. You're not going to know anything, you're going to be extremely lost and confused. You have to care enough about the language that you're working with that you can just keep on going with it even through rough patches and plateaus.

You need a *connection* to the content if you genuinely want to retain it. I find that in a lot of people, the only way for them to remember something is if they find that to some degree they care about it. This doubles up on the first point by reinforcing the idea that if you care about something, you're more likely to both work hard on it and to retain it.

You need *immersion* rather than rote memorization because immersion is going to teach you to use the language everywhere and use context to figure out new words and sounds. This is how we naturally learn our first languages and it's how we can naturally learn even more if we manage to tap into that primitive "lightbulb" notion of making things click and making gears simply turn. This builds upon the first and second points because I insist that you immerse yourself in topics that you care about, and help you to seek them out.

You need *confidence* in your ability to speak. Not in your ability to speak the *language*, you're going to be awful at the language for a long time. You need to accept that. "A long time" could be any number of measures from a month to several years. You have to realize that your reinforcement and your feedback is only going to come by speaking to people you've never spoken to before in a language that you're not entirely comfortable in. By getting out of that comfort zone and getting comfortable "being wrong", as well as by accepting that you will often flub up in seemingly simple ways, you will become a better speaker of the language even faster.

Lastly, you need *willingness* to go out of your comfort zone. This is something that only you can give yourself. I can harp on how important this and that thing is all that I want, but ultimately it's up to *you* to summon the willpower to actually make something happen for yourself in the context of language learning.

You'll need to summon a lot of willpower, in fact. This method is "fast and easy", but it's most certainly *not* a timesaver. If you want to learn a language in 10 minutes per day, you should relegate yourself to barely knowing the language in 4 years' time. If you want to learn it faster, you have to accept that your entire world will be in that language now, to the extent that you can make it so, and you have to accept that you're going to be spending an hour or two working in that language, translating both to and from, and that's not even including any time that you spend talking to your tutor.

But if you follow through with this method, I can guarantee you that you'll be a great speaker of whatever language it is that you want to speak.

Chapter 2: Break Down the Language

This is the single most important part of this entire book. Regardless of how you decide to learn after this - whether you decide to go an immersive route or a more traditional route - it will help you immensely in your journey if you break down the language that you're working with as well as language in a general sense so that you better understand exactly what you're working with.

I'd liken it somewhat to building a house on uneven land. You're going to need a *solid* foundation in place, regardless of whether the house that you build on it is in the Gothic style, the Colonial style, the Tudor style, or the Southwestern style.

The foundation of your language will be built in two parts: understanding the concepts of language *in general*, which I'm going to help you with in this chapter, as well as understanding the concepts of language *specific to your own,* which is something that's going to require some time spent in personal study and reflection on the language.

You also need this foundation in order to build whatever house you're trying to build. If you try to build a house without a foundation, it's going to fall apart. And that's truer than pretty much everything for this super immersion heavy manner of learning: if you don't set aside time in order to focus in and learn these basic building blocks of the language, you will not succeed, point blank. You will be weighed down by the intermediate difficulty of the sources you'll be surrounding yourself with and you'll fail to understand a lot of the nuance involved with the language.

See, the reason this works is because language serves a single purpose among people. It came about for one reason, and one reason solely: to communicate information. And because of this, it is very good at that specific purpose. And language offers many nuances between them all in order to discuss the caveats of a basic situation. You can take a basic phrase, sure, but you can also add a lot of detail. "The boy is tossing the ball" could become "The young boy is tossing a red ball to the dog while his mother sits on the porch and smiles."

What I'm saying is that all situations have a logical conclusion based off of the things which we can deduce about it with our own senses. As a result of this, we can surmise that all language is, indeed, intended to refer to the situations which arise around us. And indeed, language *does* serve this purpose. Because language has served a common purpose, the structures that have developed are similar as well. Our cognition reduces everything to a logical ultimate which is then expressed through words even in languages which are unrelated.

Believe it or not, most languages were once upon a time more related than they are today. Due to the patterns of conquest and migration patterns, language would actually develop both outward and inward and would change great volumes as time went on. There are a lot of reasons for this. The languages which preceded the great changes are commonly referred to as "proto-languages".

The vast majority of languages in Eurasia can be traced back to Proto-Indo-European, also called PIE. This language is by far the best understood proto-language. A huge number of languages in both Europe and Asia can be traced back to this lineage of languages. When you follow this lineage back and try to understand where and why each form departs, you're involved in what is actually a super interesting study; an inquiry into the origins and history of a great portion of language.

So because of this alone, a great number of the languages that you may desire to learn are related in some way or another, down the line. Their syntax, of course, has definitely changed in some capacity or another since those days long ago, but that's just the natural march of language. The point I'm trying to make here is that those languages have concepts in common.

And the languages which aren't related in such a manner to Proto-Indo-European will still share many of these same features, just because they're simply required in order to form a rational thought or delineate any sort of idea. So what this means is that even if you want to speak something like Mandarin Chinese or Lao or Hebrew or Arabic, they'll still share these key concepts because the singular purpose of language is to make logical inferences based off of events. At some point, every language evolved from a tribe of people needing to say things like "Let's settle here" - "You need to milk the cow" - "How can we best grow this plant?" - "There are migrating bison out to the west that we can kill." And indeed, the vast differences between multiple languages sets you up for a great number of uniformities among them.

So, this means that we can separate our language learning process into a lot of smaller and more malleable chunks that you can take advantage of and utilize one at a time in order to get a sound result.

Learn the Differences

This point can't be made enough. I've already made apparent that languages are contextually very similar. This means that if you spend a lot of time learning the similarities between a language, you're going to find a lot of them. A whole lot of them.

I know this is a really easy mistake to make, because when I first embarked on my language learning adventures, I started out by Googling "what language is the easiest for a person to learn?" My desire to be worldly and bilingual conflicted heavily with the amount of work I was truly willing to put out in return for such a thing. As I'm sure is no surprise, it didn't really work out for me.

What I should have done *instead* of learning what was within my comfort zone was ignore that another language would be out of my comfort zone entirely. There's no reason to think that, because every language will be out of your comfort zone. When you're learning another language, there is no such *thing* as a comfort zone, because every language will differ from your own (though possibly in varying degrees).

This is to say that when I say to learn the differences, I don't mean at the theoretical level; you're not at all ready for that sort of thing just yet. Instead, just do a cursory review of things such as the Wikipedia article for the language. When you do this, you'll be able to see not only the history of the language but also a few things about it. There are certain terms that will scare you or confuse you at first - for example, *agglutinative,* which means nothing linguistically to English speakers because English isn't agglutinative - but there will normally be at the very least a cursory explanation of the term within parentheses, or a link to the article on that concept itself which will normally provide both an in-depth examination and cumulative overview of the topic.

Why learn the differences before you get too into the language itself? Because that's how it works. You have to be prepared for whatever you may be facing. For example, if you were wanting to learn Chinese, it'd suit you well to know essential things which cause it to differ from English. For example, it's a tone language, as opposed to English which isn't. The meaning of words in Chinese can change drastically depending upon the tone in which you say the word. A person with bad tones in China sticks out like a sore thumb, though as a Westerner you'll probably get a pass for even trying to learn their language in the first place.

In other words, you've just got to know what to expect, or else you may find yourself completely blind-sided by a language in some ways or another. This is the last thing you want. You need to know what to expect going into the language so that you're actually prepared and not scrambling when some technique presents itself.

Now with that little aspect out of it all, it's time to move onto the technical aspects: the things you need to learn before doing anything else.

Learn the Alphabet

This seems a little terse, I'm sure. But the fact is that there are a lot of languages which don't have Latin alphabets or even anything close. Let me put it this way: there are a lot of languages which you don't understand, and there are a lot of alphabets, too, that you don't understand.

I can think of several off of the top of my head.

First, there's *Cyrillic script*, which is used heavily by Russia, though also by countries which have developed in its approximate proximity. Languages which use the Cyrillic script include but are certainly not limited to Russian, Ukrainian, Mongolian, Kazakh, and Macedonian.

Then there are the Semitic scripts like Arabic and Hebrew. You need to learn these before doing anything else, however you can. This is for the simple fact that they can be convoluted and confusing, but also because a nifty feature of these scripts is that they can completely exclude vowels and leave you to just decipher a word based upon context. This is actually a really cool linguistic model based upon triconsonantal roots, but it can be very confusing as a beginner. It becomes even more confusing when you're trying to struggle with the basic alphabet on top of that. The alphabet should without a doubt be the first thing that you learn in these languages.

Then, for example, there's the Korean script *hangul*. This is a really simple script to learn and understand, especially because it was created specifically for Korean by a single guy in order to make Korean far easier to read. However, the case here is much like a less serious version of the case for semitic scripts: the vast majority of the source material that you'll be encountering and even language-teaching guides you may encounter will invariably be written to some extent in the language itself.

This method has some shortcomings, overall. I'll admit that. It doesn't work well for logographic languages. Logographic languages are languages which, as opposed to an alphabet crafted from individual graphs which all represent a singular sound consistently, have instead a unique character for every single word in the language. A beautiful example of a logographic language is Chinese, and Japanese would be another sterling example as well (aside from Katakana). For logographic languages, the only way at all to really learn the language is to practice it. The only way around this is if you decide to learn how things sound when they're Romanized and learn the Romanized version of the language at a faster rate than you're learning the logographic characters. You can base the characters that you're learning off of the words that you already know. This is the only feasible way I can imagine taking my language learning method and applying it to logographic languages, and it's possible but will certainly be difficult due to the lack of a real wealth of Romanized resources in these languages available for you to learn by.

Learn the Structure

Once you know the alphabet, you need to learn about the structure of a language. Languages are essentially composed of three different extremely basic components: subjects, objects, and verbs. There isn't a language that lacks any of these three components. I'll explain them more in a second.

English, for reference, is a subject-verb-object language. This is massively different compared to, say, Japanese, which is a subject object verb language, or

Arabic, which is a verb subject object language.

So what does this mean exactly? This refers to the order of the given parts of speech in a conventional sentence within the language.

Subjects - Subjects are the things which the sentence is based around. However, since this can be a little vague, it's better defined as the thing which ultimately controls or is the progenitor of the verb. The reason I add the progenitor clause is because in the sentence "It is nice," the subject is still *it* because the verb *is* (a conjugated form of *to be*) has to do directly with the verb *it*. *It* is existing in such a manner, so it's acceptable to say "It is", even if "it" isn't doing anything directly with the verb "is". Subjects are also called the *nominative case* should you be working with a language which has a form or noun declension.

Verbs - Verbs are the actions which are undertaken, but they can also indicate things such as an occurrence of some sort (*to become*) or a given state (*to exist*). Verbs usually are conjugated in a certain way to their speaker, though they aren't conjugated in every language. It will vary depending mostly upon which language exactly you're speaking. But a huge number of languages have this feature, called both verb inflection and verb conjugation. All that it means is that they are changed in a certain way to agree with any number of characteristics of either the subject or the object (generally the subject), such as gender, plurality, and perspective (first person, second person, third person). Languages which are based around this concept will generally require a lot of work to understand how verbs work and how you can make them come naturally. Languages which don't have this concept make up for the difficulty elsewhere. There are actually a lot more things to verbs, such as intransitive verbs vs. transitive verbs (which pertains to whether or not they utilize a direct object), linking verbs, and so on. It really depends upon the language that you're specifically studying as to how it implements it.

Objects - Objects are the things which are on the other side of the verb. This may sound obvious and vague, but the truth is that defining objects can be a little tricky. The general definition is usually something along the lines of "the word which is affected by the verb." This can be a little tricky, however. Objects are generally divided into two classes: direct objects and indirect objects. I make this distinction in every language book I write and am certain to make the lines between them very clear. There are a lot of ways to divide and define the two, but the way that I find most useful to describe the difference between the two is by making a very clear delineation between the required nature of the two. This is to say that if you have a direct object, you can't remove it from the sentence and have it makes sense, whereas indirect objects serve a purely contextual purpose. Consider the sentence "He writes the book with me." We can divide this into its parts: "He *mails* **the book** <u>with me</u>." In this case, the subject is left unstylized, the verb is italicized, the direct object is emboldened, and the indirect object is underlined. You can see easier now the relationship between the verb and the direct object. If you were to say "He mails with me.", it would make absolutely no sense at all. People would be wondering "he mails *what* with me?" The direct object is what answers that question of *what* in sentences. However, if we were to take out the indirect object instead, like so: "He mails the book", it would make perfect sense. Indirect objects most of the time do little more than provide context. The phrase "He says it to me." is similar: the *to me*, while essential to the point of the sentence, is purely contextual and the sentence would be grammatically sound without that.

Anyhow, those are the three main components of a sentence across languages. It would serve you well to understand them all to the maximum capacity you can within your own language. Does the subject come before the verb? After? Where does the object go? Not every sentence in every language works like English sentences do. You have to remember that language has as much, if not more, societal deviation than separate cultures. The conditions which created any two given languages are never the same, and so they'll have grown differently and may have even had a completely different basis. For an example of this sort of growth, *PIE* was originally a subject object verb sentence, as were Ancient Greek and Latin. However, as they would grow and develop, they would change this order entirely. And it's not unusual for this sort of thing to happen over periods of vast linguistic growth. English, for example, dropped the idea of verb-second word order altogether.

As you read through all of this, you should be simultaneously learning *how*. This is how you're going to build your foundation: learning exactly how all of it works. You aren't going to go very far if you don't take the time to do all of this.

For subjects, it's imperative that you learn every possible subject pronoun and, a little later, every possible object pronoun. You're going to be using these and seeing these extensively for the simple reason that they're everywhere. There isn't a sentence which can work without a subject. Well, there are, but they aren't valid sentences generally. There are some sentences, such as Spanish, which allow you to drop the subject due to the conjugation, but this is for the simple reason that the subject is implied through the conjugation of the sentence. Conversely, French doesn't work in such a manner; you *have* to either say a subject pronoun or you have to mention a specific subject alongside a very specific article which denotes exactly what you're talking about. This is because all of the first-person verbs mesh together on their endings and you can only tell them apart if there's liaison involved, often. So regardless of what the specific system for subjects is within the language that you're going to be working with, it's your job to understand them to the best extent which you can.

Now, speaking in terms of verbs, I've mentioned before my disdain for classroom style vocabulary learning, and going along with that, I don't think the best way to learn verbs is in that manner. However, and that's a big however, you do need to recognize verb inflection if there is such a thing, or any other manners of recognizing verbs so that you can actually work with and understand them, as well as recognize them when they show up in the text. Additionally, you really need to learn the basic verbs, and unfortunately, there will often be a lot of irregular verbs that are completely detached from any notion of normal conjugation or declension. Even in Chinese, which has *no* verb conjugation system, there are two verbs which have a marker afterwards that is irregular. These form naturally, honestly, after a long period of language speaking. This is exacerbated by the general lack of print or text reproduction technology for most of history. Alongside the general lack of literacy came a lack of standardization, which made it rather difficult to have any sort of uniformity among the language as it would grow and develop. So the changes which would occur were very massive and sweeping, and also led to some verbs losing any sort of standardized form. Perhaps such is a bit natural after several millennia of linguistic divergence, but I digress. You're going to have to practice 1) recognizing verb inflections for regular verbs, and recognizing those verbs when they pop up in the text and 2) at the *least*, the ten most common irregular verbs for the language that you're learning (if it should have that many; some don't.)

The only other trouble you'll run into in the sphere of verbs if you do those two things is understanding idiomatic expressions, or phrases which don't mean expressly what they say they mean. An example of an idiom in English would be "it's raining cats and dogs". It's not *literally* raining cats and dogs, but it is raining quite hard if one says such a thing. With that said, though, if you follow the language acquisition tips that I outline in the chapter after this one, you should these idioms through your personal translation efforts.

When it comes to verb tenses, you don't have to know every single tense. It's worthwhile for you to learn the most common past tense and future tense if they exist, though. For example, in French, this would be the passé composé and either the simple future or the *futur proche,* meaning "close future". I use French as an example because it's the language I know best, but this applies to any given language. Some languages don't have a "past tense" verb conjugation per se and have a different way of showing past tense. Either way, you're going to need to know how to use that part of speech, as well as understand how it will show up in both speech and text.

The last thing is the object. Objects generally aren't too terribly difficult to learn across languages and are typically actually one of the easier things of understand because most of the time, they'll be composed of either a noun, an article and a noun, or a preposition and a noun. The hard part is more understanding the articles and prepositions of the language so that you can recognize the indirect objects when you see them. Some languages do bizarre things with objects, but by studying the broad concept of objects within the language, then you'll be able to start to understand.

I just mentioned articles and prepositions. I do think it's absolutely necessary that you understand articles before you go any further with your language learning. This won't apply to every language - some languages don't have what we'd commonly refer to as articles, or they have them in a far different way than we'd recognize. However, it's still worth researching and finding your answer so that you can learn as to whether the given language does have them or not. Articles are things which specify the *number* and *location* of a given noun. For example, if I were to say "I ate *a* slice of pizza", it would indicate that that I ate some non-specific piece of pizza. This is commonly referred to as an indefinite article. If I were to say "I ate *the* slice of pizza", it's implied that I'm referring to a very explicit slice of pizza, not just any slice off of the street. Maybe somebody asked me what happened to a very specific slice of pizza, and I responded in accordance. This is called a *definite* article. There are also other types of articles. "This" and "that" could be considered articles - "I ate *this* slice of pizza" refers to a specific slice which you are demonstrating, where "I ate *that* slice of pizza" means you're referring to a specific slice which is elsewhere from you. The simple correlation for this is usually "this" -> "here", "that" -> "there". Articles are essential because, especially with languages like Danish and Swedish, if you don't know them, they will almost certainly get lost in the text. It's not that they're hard to understand, but it's that if you *don't* understand them, you're at a massive disadvantage.

On a related note to articles and prepositions, you may run across the notion of "gendered" nouns. This doesn't refer to a physical characteristic so much as a linguistic development. Nouns, especially in Romance languages, which have genders have such because it produces vowel harmony, and they just happen to sound best with the articles and pronouns which would be used to reference male and female human beings. Some languages will also have a *neuter* gender which will make it an even more confusing mess. But really, it doesn't quite matter on the origin of these, what matters more is that you learn the nuances of noun gender for your particular language if such a thing exists for it.

Anyhow, the next thing that you're going to want to learn is prepositions. It's important to learn at least the most basic of prepositions, because prepositions are what allow you to express yourself on a higher level. Prepositions open the door for not only idiom but for phrases which allow you to imply or explicitly state an object's location. Prepositions in English were always explained to me in grade school as "places where a squirrel can go": a squirrel can go in, out, around, through, and so forth... it wasn't a perfect explanation and it certainly is lacking in the proper nuance, but it does fit the bill pretty well. Some prepositions are absolutely essential, such as *à* in French: it's used for both location as well as a helping article in transitive verbs and general things of that nature. You have to seriously take time to learn at least the most basic of prepositions in whatever language that you're trying to learn so that you can better know what you're working with as you go forward.

What's more is that you need to learn basic conversational phrases. This is because these vary from language to language and it can be a little bizarre trying to translate some of them directly because a lot of them have no direct translation. Some of them have been the same for centuries while other aspects of the language have changed, which can make it a really bizarre experience. So the best thing to do, really, is to learn them as their own unit. Learn things like "hello", "goodbye", "thank you", and "please", alongside how to get to a certain place and how to ask for help. The other plus side is that since you've already looked a great deal into the formation of verbs and subjects and objects, you'll be able to pick each out of the sentence and likely increase your vocabulary to a certain extent.

The last thing that you really need to focus on picking up in terms of background knowledge is learning how to ask *questions* in the given language. This, too, will vary from language to language, and rather greatly at that. But asking questions is a major part of any conducive conversation. On top of that, you're going to have to work with questions in order to ask people how to get around or for the help that you'll inevitably need.

After you've built a solid foundation and you feel like you know the most essential parts of the language well, even if your vocabulary isn't excellent, then you're ready to move forward into the immersive part of this method.

You are halfway done!

Congratulations on making it to the halfway point of the journey. Many try and give up long before even getting to this point, so you are to be congratulated on this. You have shown that you are serious about getting better every day. I am also serious about improving my life, and helping others get better along the way. To do this I need your feedback. Click on the link below and take a moment to let me know how this book has helped you. If you feel there is something missing or something you would like to see differently, I would love to know about it. I want to ensure that as you and I improve, this book continues to improve as well. Thank you for taking the time to ensure that we are all getting the most from each other.

Chapter 3: Immerse Yourself

A few years ago, I tried to learn Latin from a book. It was a rather archaic book written by a well-meaning professor sometime in the 1970s or 1980s; well, I say that, but the reality is that it was written a bit later, likely in the mid-1990s, its methodology just *seemed* so outdated. This is when I began to realize a lot of the structural problems of language learning and why people become so disenfranchised with it so fast.

We already talked in chapter one about how people tend to give up learning a language because it's just "simply not for them." When they say this, I sigh, and not for them and not out of pity, but rather out of regret that we've managed to build a manner of educating people on languages that manages not to *teach* a many people who fall into these language learning classes, but rather to have them *pass a test.*

It's my firm belief, as I've already said, that not only are people *able* to learn, but they're *made* to learn language. However, just as we tend to take the fun out of a great many things in academia, language learning itself has been relegated to being a book-y study-wrought subject rather than what it actually is: an opportunity to meet new souls that you've never met before, to talk to and intertwine with people that you normally never would have because you don't even speak the same language.

See, language learning is actually a beautiful experience. By learning a language, you're allowing yourself to see into a whole new world of culture and alternative thought. Some places are a bigger departure from your customs than others, but every single place has its own unique story. What's neat is that language not only allows you to *experience* this story, but you also get to *get* some of this story from the language itself. My favorite example of this is Spanish. Spanish is a language of a territory in heavy dispute and intrinsic conflict for centuries. In their language, you find the culture of a great numerous conquests against the Spanish, most notably by the Arabs who had taken control of Spain for some 3 or 4 centuries in the first and second millennium. This is evident in the fact that Spanish had actually adopted a huge number of words from those who had conquered them - Arabic words which would come to represent either new concepts in Spain or replace the go-to word for old concepts. Of course, these weren't entirely pervasive, but their presence is noteworthy nonetheless. If you were to open a Spanish dictionary and flip back to the opening pages, you'd see several pages of words which begin with "al", which means they were more than likely taken from Arabic, which had an article "*al*" meaning "*the*".

So how we manage to turn that into a dull classroom experience is *beyond* me. Language learning itself is little more than a door to a whole new world of experiences. Sure, the lock may be a bit difficult to figure out, exactly, but the contents on the other side of the door make it worth it.

That's beside the point, though: language is an *intrinsically social* concept. It would make absolutely zero sense if you learned a new language to talk about something that you don't care about. So why would you try to go forward with learning a language if it meant doing so in a manner which you don't care about and frankly couldn't really care *less* about? It's an absolute recipe for disaster.

What I propose to you instead is a method I've developed during my language studies which I refer to as *usage-based vocabulary learning*. There's actually another method and component to this whole lesson: *passion-based immersion*.

Let me break this down.

The idea behind this theory is rather simple: we learn best when we're actually using things that we learn. Likewise, for the vast majority of people who would be categorized as kinetic learners, they learn by active usage and reinforcement of concepts and scouring out solutions if they can't find them in the first place.

What I've developed is a far more hands-on method to vocabulary increasing than what the norm is. Note that I'm not completely disowning the concept of traditional vocabulary learning, and it can, in fact, be beneficial. Rather, what I'm decrying is the idea of using *solely* traditional vocabulary learning and taking in heaps of words and then never using them again until a long time down the road.

My train of thought in developing this was actually based off of an experience I had a while back when I was learning French, my first secondary language. I had been trodding along for a while but hardly making genuine progress. I had taken it all throughout high school and would occasionally dabble with it but didn't make a lot of sense of it. It sounds really small, but at one point I discovered that the United Kingdom equivalent to the United States word "eggplant" was "aubergine", which reminded me of the French term I'd remembered some years ago but long forgotten, or at least certainly wouldn't have been able to recall. I suppose the association between the English and the French term jarred my recollection. But at that point, I started thinking about how I remembered that word solely by making a connection, and I realized that past a certain point, the totality of language learning is the gentle art of making things click.

It seems like a rather small incident and it was, for certain - but the consequences of it, the train of thought which resulted, made me get back to learning French by way of *practicing* it. If I ever needed a word, the beauty of the information age meant that I could just go to a website and find a nearly direct translation, along with a sentence and comparative context. That was a huge boon to my ability to speak French well and I realized that I was growing quickly and had made on my own a realization that every great language learner has made: language learning, whether it be your first language or your fifth language, always occurs because you see/hear a word you don't know, analyze the context, and give that word a context. So if it works that way, I reasoned, why couldn't the opposite be true? Why couldn't we have a *context* that we didn't know how to explain, and learn the language through adjustment and effort to those given contexts? The same mechanism of making things "click" is present within both actions, so long as you know the basics of the language that the words you're presenting for your context aren't either outlandishly difficult or impossible to parse given your understanding of a language.

Anyway, having made this realization and being the aspiring poet that I was at that point, I took to writing quite a bit of poetry. This helped me greatly in learning the uses of various words I *did* know as I would research them for correctness, as well as allowing me to practice them, and it also helped me to increase my vocabulary because I had specific ideas that I was trying to convey.

That's why one of the pillars which I recommend to you as a language learner is the following: find a way to **use** your language. There is absolutely no way around this step. As a new speaker, you may feel a tad uncomfortable using it around other people, and that's okay (even though you'll have to sometime.) What I recommend that you do instead is start writing a nightly journal, recounting your day in the language which you were trying to learn, and expressing any thoughts you might have otherwise in the language as well. Do this daily, regardless of whether you're talking to people in the given language yet or not. There is no way around this task. It's simple, it doesn't take terribly long, and it's the most effective form of study that you can undertake: that which allows you to truly *express*.

There are a great number of reasons that you should take my advice and write a nightly journal in the language of your choosing. The first, of course, is that it allows you to practice the language. The second is that you're going to naturally pick up a lot more words. You'll get a lot of experience using common expressions and you'll find yourself feeling like more of a natural when it comes to things like irregular verbs or noun declension. Even things like verb conjugation will come out to be much easier for you. Write your *thoughts*, studiously, and if you ever have a question about whether a certain verb tense exists in the language you're studying, or whether a certain word exists, then I implore you to *research it*.

The truth is that you have *got* to learn vocabulary somehow. There are a lot of ways to do it. But when it comes between a method which works on our intuitive capacity to learn and utilize language, and one which just requires rote memorization of given concepts which we may or may not use at a later point, I will always opt for the first.

This is the first time that I've published this method, so my sample size is rather small; in fact, it consists solely of myself. But I genuinely believe that this specific method of acquiring new vocabulary in a language is far better than the traditional method.

As I said though, there's still a lot of room for traditional vocabulary learning in the sense of non-usage memorization techniques. In fact, as a standalone tactic, there's nothing intrinsically *wrong* with them as a primary language learning route. It's just that there's an option which is *better* as a primary language learning route, because it actively engages you. I genuinely believe that to some degree we've surpassed the archaic notions of rote memorization, because when I hear that I can't help recalling about the tutored children in Greece who were required to recite epic poems.

With that said, there is certainly and without a doubt a place for them as a *secondary* method of language acquisition, and I do certainly encourage you to use them in this manner. I believe that the most well-known example of these rote-memorization services being used as a sort of way to reinforce grammar and explore vocabulary is the *Duolingo* service available at (http://duolingo.com), though if you're learning Chinese you may be inclined to look at "Hello Chinese" (http://hellochinese.cc) which is very similar to China.

I think that grammar and vocabulary are two distinct phenomena, in a way. I think that grammar requires independent case-related study - you aren't going to remember how to form, for example, the imperfect tense in Italian if you aren't actively using it in any way - so you should research it as you need it in your personal writings and so that you're prepared to use it *next* time you need to. Basically everything about this language acquisition method is diametrically opposed to anything that requires you to memorize something *before* you run across it naturally.

In other words, I don't feel like there's anything very organic about learning a language by remembering words on a page. And likewise, I think that since it's such an inorganic method of language acquisition, I don't think that people who decide to use this specific route of language acquisition are going to go terribly far at all with it.

I know what you're thinking: "If I wait to learn these things until I need them, then how am I going to know how to use them when I need them?"

I understand that concern entirely. I will say that your basic introductions to a language should always include how to form the past tense or, in the few languages for which there isn't a specific past tense, how to indicate something happened in the past, just in case you run into a need for it. However, here are two facts:

1) When I say you need to learn things as you encounter a need to learn them, I don't mean that every time you need a word should be when you're out in the streets needing help for this or that. What I mean is that you

need to practice a direct yet detached method of language acquisition which focuses on the *organic* process of interpreting and understanding new terms as opposed to the process which focuses entirely on the sole acquisition of new terms that many language learning courses devolve into.

2) Kindness is a human trait. No matter how much people tell you otherwise, for the vast majority of people, the default will always be kindness. So if you walk into a place in a foreign country and have to fumble with the language, they won't be angry and they won't be upset with you. Learning somebody else's language is a show of *respect*, not disrespect, and they will only respect you and try to help you for learning their culture. Most people are proud of where they come from to some extent or another, and anything respect paid to the culture of where they call "home" is looked kindly upon. So there's nothing wrong with speaking a Pidgin version of a language or hardly knowing how to conjugate verbs (though this isn't realistic if you're working with the language on a nightly basis).

The reason I say all of this is to articulate why I don't think that programs like Duolingo are great if they're the *only* source that you're working with. I just feel as though they fail in an essential way. If you are working with two concepts which beg development on their own accord, then the experience of learning both is diluted.

So I'm sure at this point you're skeptical. This is a little bit of a bizarre way to learn a language, I understand. But try it and you'll understand.

Let me now move onto the other part, which will hopefully clear up any residual concerns you have about the language learning process I'm suggesting, and the reason this chapter is called "Immerse yourself".

There are two sides to immersion: *ingoing* and *outgoing*. *Outgoing* is what we just talked about: the actual private usage of the language in order to develop your ability to speak in it. This is one essential part of this paradigm of language acquisition.

The other part then is obviously *incoming immersion*. These are the influences in the language that you're taking in from the *outside*. Language learning ideally should include a beneficial balance of both of these. I frankly have yet to figure out exactly what this balance should be, though.

So what, in my eyes, makes up *incoming immersion*? Anything that you experience in the language that allows you to make sense of something. These are things which act on those "make it click" mechanisms in our brains in order to connect certain lines between words and meaning in the new language. There are a lot of ways that you can actually achieve this.

The first is rather obvious: change the language of your phone and computer to the language you're wishing to learn. This specific suggestion may work better for languages in the Indo-European language family as it's much easier to "extrapolate" the meanings of vague phrases when they have a similar formation. This is pertinent when it comes to technology because certain things *are* in longer, complete sentences, but a huge number of things are not, like application names or menus in the Windows file explorer such as "This Computer". This isn't exclusively true, however, and if you have a knowledge of how the language is written, pronounced, and structured, it's probably in your best interest to immerse yourself in that manner.

The second is obvious as well: use subtitles to your advantage. Netflix has thousands of titles streaming that are available in multiple languages, as well as a huge number of films which are available in both English and alternative language subtitles as well. This can be extremely conducive to those "make it click" mechanisms because you're actively enthralled by the thing that you're watching.

My recommendation, should you decide to go along with this, is to start with English audio and subtitles in your given language *first*. After you're comfortable with the language, I would then switch over to the audio in your given language and English subtitles. The reason for this is that it's really easy to be confused or thrown off by a language's accent at first as a language learner, and I don't think that it's ultimately very conducive to try to wean words apart in the native language and give them an English meaning from the English subtitles if you don't know very much about the language. That sort of thing is more for learning supplementary words and idioms once you have a firm enough grasp of the language in other contexts. As you're starting out, you 110% should start with English audio, just because it allows you to get used to reading the given language and acquainting the many words you don't know at that point to their English equivalent rather than the converse. The power of audio only goes so far, and in English, you already know where words start and end. As a beginner in a new language, you often don't have such a privilege.

So as we go forward with the idea of ingoing immersion, we're coming to the topic that I mentioned earlier and that I think is ultimately one of the two most important things to take away from this chapter: *passion-based immersion*.

So what do I mean by this? It probably sounds a tad pretentious, I'm aware, but the meaning is pure.

Human interests arise as forces in society as people group together in order to talk about them and join in solidarity over their admiration for the given topic. That is to say that often these topics will cross the general lines of linguistic division and carry over across languages.

What's more is that we always learn better when it's something that we care about, or connected in a way, even only tangentially, to something that we care about. We're more likely to forge mental connections and remember things which need to be remembered if they're connected to something that we ultimately care about rather than something that we, well, don't.

This theory builds upon that idea. The premise is simple: take the things you like and take advantage of that in order to learn a new language. But the manifestation can be a tad difficult.

The exact advice for carrying this out really depends ultimately upon what your passions even *are*. Regardless of what they are, the chances are much better than the converse that the region where the language you're learning is either spoken currently or has had a presence before will have *some* sort of connection to the topic.

For example, let's take World War II. A lot of people are *greatly* interested in World War II as a general topic. By learning French or Russian, you could read about the events from either a French or a Soviet perspective respectively.

I guess the point I'm trying to make in this instance is that earlier, I mentioned that learning a language opens the door to a lot of culture. Well, by this point I've already enumerated many times over how important being passionate is to the idea of language learning and how much it will help you.

So what I'm telling you to do here is to connect those two ideals of regional culture and passion in some manner so that you can find a book written in the source language that you'll actually *want* to read. Every night, translate either a page or a paragraph depending upon both how big the book is and how much time you have to dedicate to this. At first, you're going to be fumbling around a lot and encountering a lot of words you don't know - that's absolutely fine and frankly it's to be very expected. However, you should after a while make your way to the end of the book, at which point you can get another book related to your passions and repeat the process.

There are a lot of resources for translation, but I absolutely can't get enough of WordReference (http://wordreference.com). They have extensive dictionaries for a great number of languages and, on top of that, they have a wonderful system for searching up not only words but also idioms, expressions, and common phrases.

After a while, you should make your way through the book and reread it. Translate again any words that you don't understand entirely, but this time around they should be much fewer.

This will inevitably be time-consuming, but learning a language works on an inverse relationship of *effort* and *time*: the more *effort* and study that you expend towards learning a language, the less overall *time* it will take you to learn a language. So what benefits does this serve, exactly? Many!

- This method allows you to work with something that you care about. As I've already said, this makes you much more likely to internalize the information than doing it in an alternative manner.
- Working with a new language constantly will allow you to become much stronger with it.
- There's a fixed motive of finish a page/paragraph which makes it easier to go through with, but not quite laborious since you care about the topic at hand.

I think the biggest thing which makes it a great asset is the fact that you *are* mentally connected to the topic after all, though. That means that it's going to be much easier for you to absorb the words that you translate.

I don't think you need to drill yourself learning vocabulary as you're starting out, though. I think you need to focus more on patterns. Every language has patterns. For example, adverbs in English end in *-ly*; in Spanish, they end in *-mente*; in French, they end in *-ment*, and so on. So many people become disenfranchised with learning languages because it just becomes a game of constant memorization. They'll be so disheartened and stressed out by having to memorize *x* set of words, and that stress actually makes it far harder to learn.

This is where I should give yet another disclaimer: I don't think that flashcard learning methods are explicitly bad, or any other popular method of vocabulary learning. I think it can be useful if you take the right mindset about it. However, once more, I don't think it should be your primary learning vehicle. Your primary learning vehicle should be *personal experience*, no questions asked. There's nothing that will benefit you so much as immersing yourself in something that you care about.

Chapter 4: Usage

So, we're nearing the end of the book and one thing has become incredibly apparent: none of this work that you've done matters if you aren't going to find a way to use the language and reinforce the things which you've already learned.

I mean sure, reading and writing will get you to a certain extent, but what really helps a person understand a language is, frankly, *using* it. Not in journals, not in just watching the television with subtitles or dubbed audio, but with actually using the language that you've developed it.

Thanks to the things we worked on in the first chapter, I dearly hope that you're at a point where you feel confident with not only what you do know but what you *don't* know, as well as with your ability to transfer both to the real world.

The simple fact is that as you speak to other people, you are going to make mistakes, and you are going to make quite a few. But it's really not so bad; we make mistakes in our *native* language all the time, yet nobody is embarrassed about them. Think about all the people who get extremely confused on the usage differences of "your" and "you're", or of "to" and "too" and "two". People tend not to notice these -- in fact, they proclaim them proudly by virtue of not noticing them.

But the thing is that you've got to do whatever you can to get out of your comfort zone and start speaking another language. You have to actually *use* the language. Strike up conversations with new people who speak the language. If you are studying at home, not abroad, then it may benefit you to find a pen-pal or a Skype partner. There are lots of these in lots of places, I recommend *http://language-exchanges.org* in order to find people that you can converse in your new language on Skype with. However, you can also go to *http://italki.com*, which is a paid service but very popular thanks to certain personalities promoting it.

Another thing that you can do is head to *http://meetup.com*. This is a beautiful resource for meeting other people who practice the same language that you do, and generally has people who are at multiple skill levels, from beginner to intermediate to expert to fluent. All that you do is go to the site and type in your location and type in the language as the keyword. Then search. I was able to find local groups with ease. If you live anywhere near a city, as most people do, you should be able to find some group which is somewhat relevant to your interests.

The purpose in all of these things I'm suggesting is to give you the chance to practice talking under pressure, as well as to meet new people. When you meet new people who speak a different language, you can subconsciously forge a barrier with them. It's somewhat like a mask at a masquerade; you can see behind it, but why would you want to? When you meet someone under the pretense of speaking another language, you speak to them *in that language*. You can work off of each other to develop if you're at about the same level and if they're at a better level (I advise making friends with at least one person who is at a better level linguistically than you are) then you can very easily be corrected instantaneously and try to have genuine conversations with real people.

The thing too is that when you meet people in this manner, you're still meeting *people*. People with childhoods, stories, alma maters and degrees, pets and children, girlfriends and boyfriends, people who have traveled, people who were raised in a different culture, and so on and so forth. The chances are very great that if you meet a person through this method, you're going to actually *want* to talk to them in the language, which will even further drive your desire to learn the language and speak it very well.

This is one of the shortest chapters in the book, I know, but its importance can't be understated. You're doing yourself a major disservice if you opt to not try to meet others who speak the language. It's only through positive real life reinforcement that you're going to develop into a master of whatever language it is that you've decided to practice.

Conclusion

Thank for making it through to the end of *Learn Languages: The fastest and easiest way to learn any foreign language*, let's hope it was informative and able to provide you with all of the tools you need to achieve your goals whatever it may be.

The next step is to take these things we've talked about and apply them. I've made it more than abundantly clear just how you can do that. You need to be the one to go outside of your comfort zone. Use words you don't quite understand, conjugate verbs in conversation that you're not quite familiar with, do anything and everything. It is only through use and reinforcement that you'll learn a language in a short amount of time.

I genuinely hope that the help I've tried to provide throughout the course of this book is something that you've found useful. It's my sincere goal as somebody who cares very genuinely about linguistics that you may use these tips in order to become a better speaker of another language, and that you may also be exposed to the concepts which I care so dearly about.

Finally, if you found this book useful in any way, a review on Amazon is always appreciated!

Help me improve this book

While I have never met you, if you made it through this book I know that you are the kind of person that is wanting to get better and is willing to take on tough feedback to get to that point. You and I are cut from the same cloth in that respect. I am always looking to get better and I wish to not just improve myself, but also this book. If you have positive feedback, please take the time to leave a review. It will help other find this book and it can help change a life in the same way that it changed yours. If you have constructive feedback, please also leave a review. It will help me better understand what you, the reader, need to make significant improvements in your life. I will take your feedback and use it to improve this book so that it can become more powerful and beneficial to all those who encounter it.

Free membership into the Mastermind Self Development Group!

For a limited time, you can join the Mastermind Self Development Group for free! You will receive videos and articles from top authorities in self development as well as a special group only offers on new books and training programs. There will also be a monthly member only draw that gives you a chance to win any book from your Kindle wish list!

If you sign up through this link http://www.mastermindselfdevelopment.com/specialreport you will also get a special free report on the Wheel of Life. This report will give you a visual look at your current life and then take you through a series of exercises that will help you plan what your perfect life looks like. The workbook does not end there; we then take you through a process to help you plan how to achieve that perfect life. The process is very powerful and has the potential to change your life forever. Join the group now and start to change your life!
http://www.mastermindselfdevelopment.com/specialreport

You will also love these other great titles from Mastermind Self Development!

You will want to check out these other great titles Mastermind Self Development. All available in the Kindle store or you can just click on covers below.

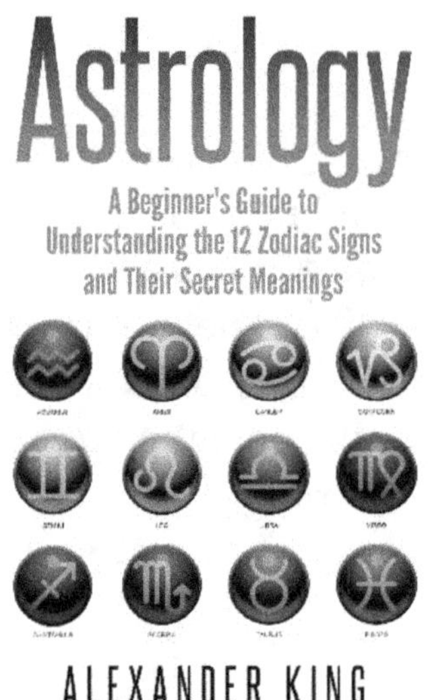

http://getbook.at/AstrologyBeginner

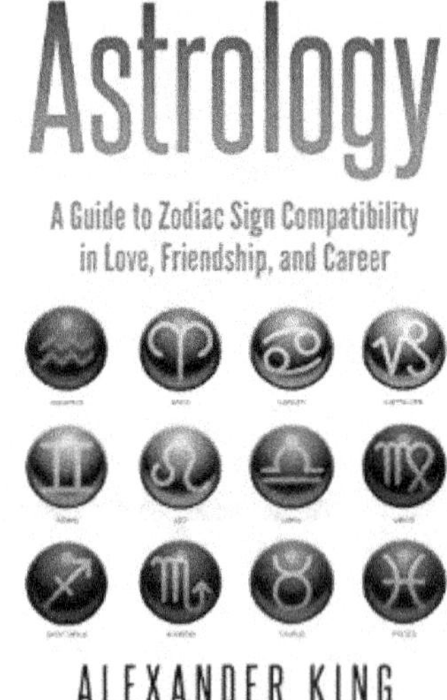

http://getbook.at/Astrologyguide

You can also find these titles by searching them in the Kindle store on Amazon.